現代建築家コンセプト・シリーズ27

ドットアーキテクツ｜山で木を切り舟にして海に乗る

JN077069

LIXIL出版

Projects

p. 100   Search Project vol. 4: *New "Colony/Island"—Art, Science and Spirit of the "Island"*
Project members: Masahiro Ueda (Professor, Graduate School of Science, Osaka University), Toshiyuki Nakagaki (Professor, Research Institute for Electronic Science, Hokkaido University), dot architects (architect unit), yang02 (artist), Takanobu Inafuku (artist, programmer)
© Art Area B1, 2015. Photo by Nobutada Omote

p. 102   Railway Art Festival vol. 5: Closing Event "Alternative Train of the Future"
Director: Takashi Homma
Performers: NAZE, Yuya Koyama, PUGMENT, dot architects, Ryu Mieno, contact Gonzo
© Art Area B1, 2015. Photo by Yoshikazu Inoue

Photographs

Yusuke Nishimitsu   Cover
JP/ p. 9–24, 31, 34, 40, 41, 47, 52, 56, 57, 60, 61, 67, 70, 72, 73, 76, 83, 89
EN/ p. 9–24, 26, 28, 31, 32, 35, 38, 40, 42, 45, 47, 48, 50, 54, 56

Takuya Matsumi   p. 101 contact Gonzo: *Gonzo Kaitai Shinsho* 13-minute Azumaya

Hideaki Hamada   p. 104 UmakiCamp

Yoshikazu Inoue   p. 101 KYOTO EXPERIMENT 2017: Yudai Kamisato/Okazaki Art Theatre, *The Story of Descending the Long Slopes of Valparaiso*

p. 102 Railway Art Festival vol. 5: Closing Event "Alternative Train of the Future"

Nobutada Omote   p. 100 Search Project vol. 4: *New "Colony/Island"—Art, Science and Spirit of the "Island"*

dot architects   all other photos

Contemporary Architect's Concept Series 27

dot architects | Cut Trees on the Mountain, Make a Boat, Float It on the Sea

First published in Japan on October 1, 2020 by LIXIL Publishing

LIXIL Publishing
2-1-1 Ohjima, Koto-ku, Tokyo, 136-8535, Japan
TEL: +81 (0)3 3638 8021   FAX: +81 (0)3 3638 8022
http://livingculture.lixil.com/en/publish/

Author: Toshikatsu Ienari
Publisher: Jin Song Montesano
Planning and Editing: Mutsumi Nakamura, Jiro Iio (Speelplaats Co., Ltd.)
Text Translation: Alan Gleason
Design: Minori Asada (MATCH and Company Co., Ltd.)
Printing: Kato Bunmeisha Co., Ltd.

© 2020 by dot architects

All rights reserved.
No part of this book may be reproduced or utilized in any information storage and retrieval system, without prior permission in writing from the copyright holder.

Printed in Japan ISBN978-4-86480-048-8 C0352

●目次

家成俊勝（ドットアーキテクツ共同代表）

日々の暮らしは変化し続けている。私たちの身のまわりには、あらゆるものがレイアウトされていて、何百年単位でゆっくり変わるものから、季節によって、あるいは昨日と今日で違う無数のものが私たちを囲んでいる。山や川、高速道路や鉄道、住宅、テーブル、その上に散らばるクッキーの粉まで、周到に計画されたものから、気まぐれなものまでさまざまである。さらに私たちは家、学校、職場、町内会、ネットサークルなどさまざまなグループに同時に参加していて、その参加密度はバラバラ。人は移動したり居座ったり、考え方も変わったり変わらなかったり。私たちはいつもこの配置や関係性のなかにある。建築は容易に変わらないものを手がかりに設計していくのが常道であるが、動的な状態、日々新しく生まれる出来事そのものに反応していく手立ても考えたい。「いま、ここ」にあるもの、「いま、ここ」に欲しいもの。

私たちは、国や地方公共団体から与えられるサービスを受け取る身体に慣らされている。それは私たち自身が、私たちの空間をつくることを疎外しているとも言える。また、立法爆発と言われるほど新しい法律ができていることに現れているように、私たちを取り巻くさまざまなことはもはや専門家

と言われる人にしか読み解けない複雑なものになっている。理解できないことが前提となり、私たちはつねに受け手に回ることになる。仕組みや空間は上から降ってくるものではない。地べたから生えるものだ。私が暮らす地べたがあり、その地べたが連なり、私たちの日々の生活がある。

ドットアーキテクツの仕事の特徴のひとつは一般的な建築設計だけにとどまらず、施工や、イベント企画、アートプロジェクトへの参加、パフォーマンス、スペース運営など多岐にわたることである。時間的にも、長く建っているものから一時的に建って壊されるもの、たった20分程度で終わるものもある。仕事の種類、時間の長短はあれど、これらはいずれなくなるので、一旦、これらをすべて仮設のものとして捉えるのはどうだろうか。それはさまざまに溢れる予測データ、押しつけられる未来を拒み、建築の自律性を謳うわけでもなく、意思を持って「いま、ここ」に反応してグニャグニャと戦術を変えていくサーファーのノリである。アンケートやマーケティングといった手法で、つくり手と受け手を分け、さらにその受け手を十把一絡げに扱うようなことはせず、個別の出来事や、個々に起

き上がる波に焦点を合わせ、社会においてこれが正しいと誰もが言うことは無視して、特異性や変態性とその妥協点を発見し、そこにアプローチしていきたい。

広島大学大学院社会科学研究科准教授の松嶋健さんの『プシコ ナウティカ——イタリア精神医療の人類学』（世界思想社、2014）という本に、イタリアで精神病院を廃絶した運動が紹介されている。その運動では「Da vicino nessuno è normale（近づいてみれば誰一人まともな人ないない）」というスローガンが使われていた。

何がまともなのか。何が正しいのか。それは社会という見えない主体の集合ではなく、それぞれが生きている場所から、それぞれの理屈で起き上がってくるもののせめぎ合いのなかにあるのだと思う。

猪瀬浩平さんの『むらと原発——窪川原発計画をもみ消した四万十の人びと』（農山漁村文化協会、2015）のなかで取り上げられている、原田津さんという方の言葉を紹介する。

　──「いたずら」に会合を重ね、「いたずら」にもみ、「まあまあ」で妥協する。それならハナからいい──あんばいにあつらえれば──と考える人もあるかもしれないが、それはむらを知らない人のいうこ

と。むらにとって、妥協はもんだあとにだけ存在する。逆にいえばもみっぱなしではなくて、もめば必ず妥協の知恵が出てくる。妥協ということばの、いまの使われ方からすれば、これは妥協ではなくて「譲る」ということかもしれない。(…中略…)

あきらめて納得する。まあしかたないだろうなという納得である。このあたりが、なんとも都会のセンスではわからない。「どうでもいい」ともちがう。「かってにしろ」ともちがう。「地頭に勝てない」のでもない。あえていえば、あきらめなければこれからむらとしてお互い一緒に暮らしていけないではないか、それは困る、ということになる。これを聡明さと言ったら不都合だろうか。

私が建築を勉強し始めた頃、設計課題の発表の際に私という主語を使うなと散々言われた。「私が好きだから」「私がこう思っているから」、と言ったときの「私の世界」は狭く閉じていて他者と共有できないからであり、私の考えだけで建築を設計するという思い上がりへの警告である。しかし本書では私の体験をベースに話が始まっていくものが多い。その体験は埒外で起こる小さな出来事である。

その小さな出来事を私が経験した私的なものとして閉ざすのではなく、そこに、私たちが、すでに布置されたものを乗り越え、自ら生み出す空間のためのヒントを見つけ出そうとしている。私の見聞きした話は、すべてに話の筋というものがあるわけではないのだが、その筋なき筋を勝手に解釈し、筋を下支えする考えに思いを巡らすことで、私の世界とあなたの世界を繋げ、その想像力をもって物理的な空間に向かっていく。私たちの日常に起こるさまざまな出来事は掴みきれない感覚や感情、その場しのぎ、思いつきや楽しみなどのなかにあり、そこにも建築に向き合うヒントがあり、潜伏しているその場所の使い方を見つけ、可能性を広げることができる。地べたに私たちが存在していること、まさにそのことがとても面白いのだと思う。

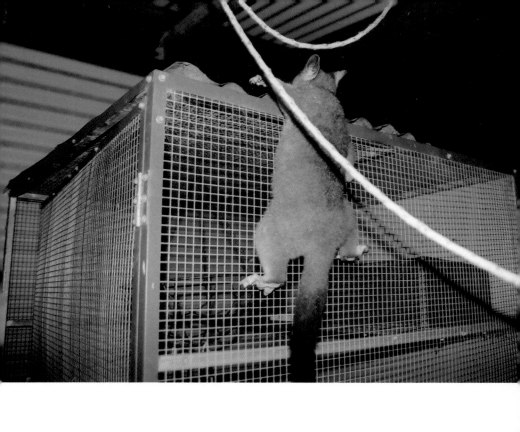

六甲の集合住宅

私は兵庫県にある六甲山の麓で生まれ育ったので、子どもの頃の遊び場は家の後ろにある山だった。学校終わりに友達と山に出かけては、道なき道を登っていき、枯葉が積もる斜面を転がり下り、その辺にある朽木や枝などを使って友人たちと山の中にボロい小屋をいくつかつくっていた。私たちは草庵のオーナーで、山は庭みたいなものだった。その山に安藤忠雄さんが設計された《六甲の集合住宅Ⅰ》が建っていた。有名な建築家が設計したものだと聞かされた。山にへばりつくコンクリートの建物がまわりにある建物と明らかに違っていることは子どもながらに明白だった。その時分に、それが格好良いとか悪いとかいう美意識や、設計者や工事関係者の苦労を考える想像力はなかったが、ただ何か不気味で異質な砦のようなものがドンと立ち上がったという感覚の記憶はある。

ある日、そんな山の木が伐採され、私たちのボロ小屋は強制撤去され、《六甲の集合住宅

Ⅱ》の建設工事が始まった。遊び場を奪われ、恨めしく山を眺める毎日だったが、中学生になって山で遊ぶ年頃でもなくなり、しばらくして《六甲の集合住宅Ⅱ》ができあがった。

当時住んでいた借家の隣の家が、ある日取り壊されて駐車場になった。見通しが良くなったトイレの小窓からは、小便をするたびに網戸越しにいつも《六甲の集合住宅》が見えた。今思えば、建築に関わる仕事をするスタート地点はここにあったのだと思う。

高校生の頃から幼馴染みの父親が働く工務店で時々アルバイトをさせてもらい、建設現場をまわってゴミを集めたり、材料を運んだり、コンクリートの打設や解体の手伝いをしていた。大学生の頃には、中学校の同級生の旦那が切り盛りする会社でお世話になって鉄筋工のアルバイトをしていた。真夏に泥と汗にまみれて地中梁の鉄筋を組んでいるうちに、日銭を稼ぐことに必死になっていたので、《六甲の集合住宅》は記憶の奥に引っ込み、建築＝施工現場と思うようになっていた。大学卒業を間近に控え、就職活動をしている最中にバブルが崩壊し、会社で働くより自分で何かつくり出す仕事がしたいと思いつつ、なかなか動き出さずにせっせと神戸のバーに通って酔いどれ生活を送っていた。当時そのバーで働いていたバーテンダーが強烈な個性を持った方々で、酒や音楽やファッションなどさまざまな情報がバーの中で飛び交っていた。たった奥行き50㎝のカウンターを挟んだ空間に、

漁師、企業の社長、ただの阪神ファンなどなど、脈絡も繋がりもない人が隣り合わせで座り、カルチャーから噂話から下世話な話まで、いろいろな情報が飛び交っていてとても面白かった。バーテンダーのひとりが、かつて大学で建築を学んでいた人で、ある日その方に、「お前建築って知ってるか？」と聞かれた。私はずっと現場で働いていたので、もちろん知っていると答えた。そこで渡されたのが『Anywhere──空間の諸問題』（磯崎新、浅田彰、NTT出版、1994）という本で、家に帰って読み始めた。が、一行も書いてあることがわからない。何が諸問題なのか全然理解できなかった。本といえばたまに読む小説くらいだった私にとってそれは衝撃的な体験で、そこから建築というものの広がりに興味を持ち始め、再び安藤忠雄さんに回帰していく。建築をやろうと決めて夜間の専門学校に通い、バーテンダーとして働きながら《六甲の集合住宅》を何度となく見に行った。斜面中腹の階段に座り、頭の上から海の方へ伸びる梁づたいに遠くを見ていた。安藤忠雄さんのディテール集を買って舐めるように見ていた。その本のなかに《六甲の集合住宅》が掲載されており、その全景を引きで押さえた写真が大きく使われていたが、その一番手前に写っている瓦葺きの洗濯物を干している家が、今はなき私の生まれ育った借家だった。たしかスペインの建築雑誌『エル・クロッキー』にもこの写真は使われていたと記憶している。ベランダに干

されたパンティーが写っていると母親に伝えると、私のではないと言い張るので少し言い合いになった。実家を出てしばらく経って、何かのおりに六甲へ帰ってきたとき、子どもの頃に入院したことのある病院が安藤忠雄さんの設計した建築に建て替わっていた。私の生まれ育った場所は、ひとりの建築家のデザインによって長い年月をかけて変貌していき、その過程とともにあったと言ってもいい。建築はそこで暮らす人々の生活を、良きにつけ悪しきにつけ大きく変えるほどの力を持っている。建築をやり始めた頃、建築なんて暴力だといろいろな人に言われたのを今でも覚えている。そういったことに無自覚になるのではなく、暴力性を引き受けたうえで何ができるか考えたい。

建築家が設計した山に立ちはだかる格好良い建築、子どもの頃につくった、風が吹いたらすぐ飛んでしまうような山の中のボロ小屋、いろいろな人と話をし、経験を共有できるバーのような居場所、そんなものが今も設計や施工を行う根底にある。

都市のワイルド

私の暮らしていた借家の隣に、めぐちゃんという1つ年下の女の子が住んでいた。ときどきその家に遊びに行ったりもしたが、他人の家はなぜ自分の家とこんなにも匂いが違うのだろうと不思議に思ったのを覚えている。私の家の2階の窓からは、めぐちゃんの家の2階と瓦屋根が見えた。春や秋の気持ちのいい季節、何気なく窓を開けると、屋根の上でめぐちゃんが本を読んでいた。屋根に寝転がって本を読む少女の姿がとても印象に残っている。めぐちゃんはやんちゃだったので、おばあちゃんに椅子にくくりつけられて怒られていたそうである。私は友達と家の前の車道で野球をして遊び、なぜか6階建のマンションの縦樋を伝って上下の移動を行い、暗渠の中を四つん這いで探検していた。溝の石垣の中には小

遣いを隠していた。ものや空間には使用する目的があるが、子どもの頃はそれらを読み替え、脱線させてもっと自由に使っていた。

批評家、翻訳家の高祖岩三郎さんは『死にゆく都市、回帰する巷──ニューヨークとその彼方』(以文社、2010)のなかで都市を構成する要素を「楼閣」と「巷」の2種に分けている。「楼閣」とは巨大建築や高速道路、鉄道網、発電所など、現代の私たちの生活を下支えしている基盤施設のことで、国家や資本によってつくられているものである。「巷」とは、さまざまな人が集まり、その関係性が活性化したような状況のことを指している。「巷」の語源は「道の股」であると言われていて、道が分岐している地点、つまり辻や岐路のことを言い、

人が往来し出会いや別れとともに賑やかさが生まれる場所でもある。現在、ストリートをはじめとする公共空間からそういった神出鬼没の「巷」が少なくなっているのは残念だが、「巷」へのアプローチを続けつつ、身体を使って「楼閣」の別の使い方を実践していけないだろうか。「楼閣」の「巷」化である。わかりやすいのはスケートボードであるが、そのほかにも建築や工作物の間を身体ひとつで飛び交うパルクールや、走る電車を波に見立て電車の屋根に乗って技を繰り出すトレインサーフィン。アーティストのマティアス・ヴェルムカ&ミーシャ・ラインカウフにいたっては、手づくりのトロッコで鉄道線路を走ったり、大きな橋梁にブランコを吊り下げて乗ったりすることで「楼閣」と身体の関係を拡張している。

自分の身体ひとつで「楼閣」に介入して状況を変える契機になるような実験的なプロジェクト《researchlight》(2016)を行った。これは「KYOTO EXPERIMENT 京都国際舞台芸術祭 2016 SPRING(以下KEX)」において、デザインスタジオ UMA / design farm とともに出展したインフラをテーマにした作品である。現在の私たちにとってインフラは、どこにでも当たり前に存在しているがゆえに、まるでGoogleの検索エンジンのような全貌が見えないシステムとなっている。そうしたインフラが「楼閣」として私たちの日常生活の多くを規定している。KEXの会場のひとつである「ロームシアター京都」は、京都の東のエッジ岡崎地区に位置し、そこは、平安時代からさまざまな時代の動乱の煽りを受けてきた場所である。平安時代に都市化され、応仁の乱によって焦土と化し、江戸時代には藩邸が立ち並んで賑わったが、幕末の動乱で再び焦土となった後に、琵琶湖疏水の通り道となり近代産業と一体になって開発されていった。そういった歴史の厚みのなかに、インフラやその名残が多く存在している。そういったインフラをいくつか選び、実測調査を経て、それらを1/1で再現してローム・スクエアという公共の中庭に設置した。選択したインフラは、疏水にあるダム、橋、配電箱、法勝寺の名残の石垣、平安神宮の屋根と鳥居の一部、歩道の手すり、野球場のスコアボード、かつて立っていた八角九重塔の基壇石、U字溝などである。これらは都市のなかに役割を持って存在しているわけだが、このプロジェクトは、インフラがコ

ンテクストや使用目的と切り離され、純粋な形として存在していたなら、人はどのようにそれらを使用するかという実験である。カットアップされた1／1のインフラは、結果的には子どもに占拠されることとなった。平安神宮の屋根は滑り台となるのにちょうどいい勾配でできており、休日になれば子どもの上に子どもが積もっていく始末である。子どもたちの動きを観察し、会期中にはインフラを改変して、パフォーマンスやスケートボーダーに使ってもらいながら、より多様な活動を引き出そうと試みた。

本書では、写真家の西光祐輔さんが撮りためていた写真や新たに撮影してもらった写真を載せているが、西光さんが長年撮り続けている対象として、都市に暮らす動物がある。西光さん本人は恥ずかしそうに「都市のワイルド」だと言っていたが、そこには都市環境を利用して生き抜く野生が写し出されている。私の生家も山に近いとはいえ住宅地であり、そのなかで、さまざまな動物と出会うことがあった。家の天井裏にはネズミが家族で暮らしていたが、ネズミは家賃も食費

も払っていない。猪の家族が庭の球根をほじくり返して食べていることもあった。さまざまな鳥もいたし、猿も家の庭の藤棚の上に出没していた。近くの家では池の鯉がアライグマに全滅させられた。同じ小学校に通っていた友達の家ではワニを飼っていたが、そのワニが逃げ出し、溝にいるワニを発見した人が通報してニュースになった。ワニは動物園に引き取られ、飼っていた家族は動物園でワニの名前を呼んでいたという。動物たちは人がつくったものの目的なぞはお構いなしで、それぞれが生き抜くために目の前にある環境を読み解いて利用して生きている。私たちは生きているうちに、身のまわりにあるものの目的が刷り込まれていく。誰かが企図した目的に対して無批判に反応するというわけではなく、その企図を乗り越えるために、さまざまな動物に成り代わるようにして違う思考と技術をもって環境にアプローチしたい。平安神宮の前を通るたびに屋根を滑る子どもたちを妄想する。平安神宮の上で本を読んでいためぐちゃんに教えてもらったことである。

以前住んでいた家で、トイレのタンク内の排水パイプの蓋をするパーツがちぎれてしまい、一度流すと水が止まらなくなったことがある。なので水を流すたびに、タンクに手を突っ込んで排水パイプに蓋をしていた。とても古い型のトイレなのでそのパーツはもう販売されていないと思う。トイレのタンクが壊れる4カ月ほど前に、洗濯機の給水が極端に遅くなってしまい、鍋に水を汲んで洗濯機の中に入れていたため、キッチンと洗濯機が置いてあるベランダを往復する始末であった。その後、ついに洗濯槽に水が貯まらなくなってしまったため、洗濯物をバスタブで手洗いし、脱水のためだけに洗濯機を利用していた。最後には脱水機能も壊れてしまい、バスタブで洗った洗濯物を手で絞って干していた。

広島大学大学院社会科学研究科准教授で文化人類学者の松嶋健さんに聞いた話だが、イタリアの哲学者ジョルジョ・アガンベンが『裸性』（岡田温司＋栗原俊秀訳、平凡社、2012）のなかで哲学者ゾーン゠レーテルの「壊れたものの哲学」を取り上げている。日本人は、電車やバスの遅延、日常的に使用しているモノが壊れたりすると、イライラする

人が大半だと思われるが、ナポリ人（もちろん全員ではないと思うが）は、何の破綻もなくシステムがすべてスムースに動いている状態に苛立ちを覚えるらしい。後者の苛立ちの根源はどこからくるのか。私が思うに、ある仕組みに対して自分の身体や思考がコミットできずにいると、「そこにいる」という実感が希薄になるのではないか。

つまり、壊れている状態というのは、そこに自分の身体やアイデアの介入の余地がある状態であり、スムースなシステムに対しては余地の不在に苛立ちを覚えるのではないか。その余地に介入するときに自ら「つくる」行為が生まれる。キューバでも同様の事例がある。キューバ革命によって親米政権が打倒された後の1961年、アメリカ大統領ドワイト・D・アイゼンハワーは、キューバとの国交を断絶させた。それにともない、アメリカ人エンジニアはキューバから引き上げ、友好国であったソ

ビエト連邦が崩壊した後には、キューバにおける物資の欠乏はさらに深刻化した。そのような状況下で、キューバ人は、破損した箇所を継ぎ当てて壊れたものを修理したり、ある製品の部品を別の機械へとつくり変えたりするなど、つくることを学んだ。金属製の椅子の座面で肉を焼き、車の底を塞いで舟にし、自転車に簡単なエンジンとペットボトルのガソリンタンクをつけバイクに改造していたそうだ。1992年には改造、修理、再利用など生活者の知恵を集めた本『With Our Own Efforts』〈自助努力〉を軍が出版し、つくることの知恵を多くの人で共有した。そこにはグレープフルーツの皮で代用してつくるステーキの調理法なども記されていたそうだ。このような物資の欠乏が多くのアマチュアエンジニアやアマチュア発明家を生み出した。

現在の私たちは、つくることに直接関わることがとても少なくなっている。多くの人が暮らす賃貸物件は、退去するときに原状回復させることが条件になっており、転居したときの状態を保持すべく、住処に対してよそ者のように遠慮することになり、場所と身体の関係はどこかギクシャクする。電化製品や車においては、現在はコンピューターが内蔵されているために自分で修理することが難しくなっているのも事実だが、それでなくても自分で何かを修理する機会はほとんどなくなっている。少し壊れれば捨てて次を買う。工業化・産業化の後に私たちに残ったのは、人間との関わりやコミュニケーションのみに注力し、モノの仕組みにコミットしようとしない情けない身体なのかもしれない。イタリア人やキューバ人、戦後を生き抜いた日本人もそうであるが、自分でいっちょやってみようというメンタリティを持つことが大切である。

二〇一五年に新潟市で開催された「水と土の芸術祭」の一環で、潟の小島に渡るための橋をつくった。つくる前に現地へ調査に行った際、福島潟の際に立つビニルハウスで活動する市民団体の方たちの集会にお邪魔した。建築家やアーティストが芸術祭だからといって突然招聘され、作品や建築などをつくるわけなので、地元の方々にとっては期待よりも心配のほうが多かっただろう。ビニルハウスの中で熊のコラーゲンや潟の小魚をいただきながら、いろいろとお話を聞いていると、「潟は何もないのが一番きれいだから余計なものはつくるな」と言われた。たしかに福島潟は渡り鳥の越冬地となっており、本当に美しいところである。建築のようなものは邪魔になるかもしれない。市民団体の内のひとり、ゴットさんが「舟をつくるのはどうか」と言ってくれたことをきっかけに、その場で舟をつくることに決めた。

　福島潟周辺には、低湿地が散在し、大小無数の水路が水田や集落の中に走っていた。このため、水路が道路の役目をし、川舟は重要な交通用具であった。（…中略…）耕地の乾田化や陸上交通の発達により潟端の生活が変わったので、川舟もしだいにその姿を消してゆき、現在では潟内での漁などでわずかに使用されるだけとなってしまった。

（『豊栄市民俗調査報告書1　豊栄の川舟──川舟の造船工程』1987）

とあるように、かつては川舟が盛んにつくられていたことがわかる。舟のつくり方を尋ねると、伝統的な舟をつくれ

る舟大工は町に1人しかいないことを教えていただいた。さっそく会おうとしたが、忙しくて無理とのことで、伝統的な舟づくりは即刻諦めた。なぜなら、ゴットさんたちも川舟をつくっていたのだが、伝統的な舟づくりにこだわらず、現代のホームセンターで売っているブチルテープやコーキング、ゴムシートをふんだんに使って舟をつくっており、私たちにはそっちのほうが面白いと思えたからだった。ゴットさんは元大工で、建築に使われる資材を舟づくりに持ち込んでいた。私たちに一級品のスキルは必要ない（もちろん大切なのは言うまでもないが）。伝統にこだわらずその場に応じて、材料を調達して工夫で乗り切るほうが性に合っている。早速、ゴットさんたちに弟子入りを志願し、2015年6月にドットアーキテクツのメンバー土井亘が福島潟に乗り込み、10日間ほど修行して現代版川舟のつくり方を習得して帰ってきた。大阪にあるドットアーキテクツの事務所で長さ8mの川舟を3艘つくり、新潟に送って潟に浮かべた。それらを繋ぎ、小島へ渡れる橋として福島潟に新しい散策コースをつくった。現場を去るときに、ゴットさんは土井に愛用の鉋（かんな）をプレゼントしてくれた。今もいろいろな現場で、土井が大切に使っている。

私たちはどこか勝手に、いつも触れているジャンルと違うものには手を出せないと思っている節がある。今回、まさか舟をつくることになるとは思ってもみなかったが、やればできるものだ。いっちょやってみようというメンタリティには、専門化された特殊技能よりも、ホームセンターの資材や、不足を自分たちで補ったり、壊れたものを自分たちで繕う技術が合っている。つくった舟はその後、1艘は市民団体の方々に使ってもらい、別の1艘は青木淳さんが設計した潟博物館のアプローチにそっと置かれている。もう1艘はどこにいったかわからない。

私は神戸の六甲山の麓に建つ借家に、両親、弟、父方の祖母と6人で暮していた。その借家は昭和初期、阪急電鉄の路線拡大に合わせて建てられたものだと思うが、建った当時は野中の一軒家だったと聞いている。当時の大工が洋風建築を真似て建てた擬洋風の木造2階建だった。私が住んでいたとき借家はすでに古くなっており、木製建具の建て付けは悪く、あらゆる窓と窓枠の間に隙間があった。冬場は隙間風でカーテンが揺れ、家の外のほうがまだ暖かいのではといつも思っていた。風の強い日は、家のあちこちからずっと音が鳴っていて、まるで家族以外の何かが一緒に住んでいるような、あるいは何かがつねに家に入ったり出たりしているようで、子どもの頃は怖かったのを覚えている。縁側には蟻が行列をつくり、部屋にはナメクジが這い、天井裏ではネズミが走り、ムカデや蜘蛛やヤモリやいろいろな生き物が家の中にいた。家の中に蔦も侵入していた。私が大学生

のときに祖母が亡くなり、葬儀を済ませた数日後に祖母が暮らしていた押入れがついた四畳半の部屋を掃除していた。その部屋も類にもれず窓と窓枠に隙間があり、雨がよく吹き込んだのであろう、クシャクシャに丸めた紙が窓と窓枠の間に詰め込まれ、止水パッキンとして使われていた。その丸まった紙を手に取り、何の気なしに広げた私の母が唖然とした顔をしていた。その紙は私の父親の卒業アルバムの1ページだったのである。やむにやまれぬ理由があったときに、あるいはそこにあるモノの配置や特性だけを純粋に見たときに、家族の大切な記憶や特性の欠片であろうが、使えるものは使うという姿勢が清々しい。そこにあるものを、そこで暮らす人のために、そこで使う。私たちが生活するために必要な資源のレイアウトは決まっている。遥か遠くの場所で掘られた石油や鉄鉱石などを資源として移動させるために、生活者には触れることのできない複雑なシステムができあが

る。私たちの生活は目の前にある材料を使わず、そんなシステムによって差し出されたものを使う毎日である。つまり、卒業アルバムの紙は使える素材だと言っているのではなく、ほんの身近にあるあらゆるモノを材料や食料だと捉えることができるかどうかである。

ところで国土交通省の「道路統計年報2019」によると、日本の道路部の面積は7710㎢あるらしい。静岡県に近い面積である。すべてとは言わないが道路のアスファルトを剥がして食料や資材を育てる場に変えれば、と妄想してしまう。

イタリアには「社会センター」という自主管理によるオルタナティブスペースが多くあるそうだ。空き家や閉鎖した施設を不法占拠してつくられた場所で、地域の人が集まり、図書館や語学教室、護身術の教室、レストラン、カフェなどを自律的に運営している(北川眞也「イタリア・ミラノにおける社会センターという自律空間の創造――社会

的包摂と自律性の間で」『都市文化研究 第14号』、2012)。もちろん立ち退きなどの憂き目にあうこともあるようだ。「社会センター」は、すぐ近くにある誰も使っていない場所をなぜ使ってはいけないのか、という素朴な疑問が出発点にあると思う。

ドットアーキテクツは「瀬戸内国際芸術祭2016(夏会期)」に小豆島の坂手地区で行われたクリエイターズレジデンスに参加した。すでに作品を展開する敷地は決まっており、坂の途中に造成された小さな納屋のついた空き地であった。そこに山と海を繋ぐ木道をつくることにした。以前、東北大学災害科学国際研究所の川島秀一教授から「暇さえあれば手紙でも待つように海を眺める習慣がある」(田辺寿男『海辺――高知の民俗写真1』、高知市民図書館、1993)という言葉を教えてもらった。海辺に暮らす人たちの真理をついた言葉である。かつての海際の集落というのは、海から家屋、山までがひとつの連なりのなかにあり、ズルズルと

繋がっていたのである。その後、戦後復興から高度成長期にかけて、物流のために設けられた沿岸の道路と併せて、安全を確保するための防潮堤が施設された。それによって経済発展と自然災害からの防衛は成し遂げられたが、同時に山と海の連関が断ち切られた。そして今、再び海や大地との関係を結びなおし、いつぞやの計画者のアレンジメントを乗り越えたいという思いから、高台から海へと続く木道をつくることにした。海をテーマにした素晴らしい文章はいくつもあるが、柳田國男の『海上の道』(角川文庫、2013)では寄物の話が出てくる。

我々は国内の山野が、かつて巨木の樹木をもって蔽われ、それが次々と自然の力によって、流れて海に出ていた時代を、想像してみることが出来なくなっている。以前は水上から供給する物が、今より遥かに豊かだったと思われる。

——多くの沖の小島では、各自昔からの神山を抱えながら、それには慎んで斧鉞を入れず、家を建てるにも竈の火を燃すにも、専ら大小の寄木を当てにしていた時代が久しく続いた。

海から流れついた多くのものを暮らしに必要な材料として使うために拾得していた生活を描いている。今福龍太さんによる文章「群島響和社会〈並行〉憲法 断章」(《流球共和社会憲法の潜勢力 群島・アジア・越境の思想》未来社、2014)では「放擲」という概念が出てくる。領土を占有することで所有の概念が生まれた。一方「放擲」は、所有を下敷きにした共有ではなく、放棄でもなく、放たれているが、配慮をもって並存するような、間借りするような、そんな意味で使われていると思う。この「拾得」と「放擲」にはどちらも、人間より先に大地や海が据えられていて、環境を人間の力によって改変していくのではなく、大きな有機物も無

機物も含めた自然のなかに人間が在るということ
を意識させてくれるものだ。「手紙でも待つよう
に」と言っているように、かつて人間は、海から
くる人や物などの寄物を待ちつつ、手紙を送るよ
うに海へと人や物を見送ったに違いない。このプ
ロジェクトでは、裏山から木材を切り出し、皮を
剝いて、生木のまま杭や横架材として利用した。
床材はいつぞやの難破船の床板である。つくった
のは小さな木道だが、目線の先に海が見え、振り
かえると山が見える、そのような自然の連関を感
じつつ、そこにある材料に一手間かけてその場で
使うことの意味を考えさせられた。また現在、日
本の林業は厳しい状況にある。戦後の住宅不足を
補うために、広葉樹林を切り開き、建築材料とな

る杉と檜が国の政策で植えられた。そして工業化
や産業化が進んだ経済成長期には、山間部から都
市部への出稼ぎ労働者が増え、都市部の労働賃金
の上昇につられるかたちで林業従事者の賃金も上
がった。固定相場制から変動相場制に代わったこ
とで海外から安い木材が入ってくるようになり国
内産の材木の需要が減っていく。木を使いたいと
思ったときに原木市場に行って木を買おうとする
とだいたいは断られる。すぐそこに、まさに山の
ように建築資材が生えているのに、その資材がま
わらないのは不思議である。そこにあるものを、
使うことができない。
そこで暮らす人のために、使うことができない。
その厄介な理由を考えるたびに父親の卒業アルバ
ムを思い出すのである。

何かをつくろうと思うと必ず道具が必要になってくる。イヴァン・イリイチという哲学者が『コンヴィヴィアリティのための道具』（渡辺京二＋渡辺梨佐訳、ちくま学芸文庫、2015）という本のなかで、ものをつくるための道具を2つに仕分けしている。1つは産業主義的道具。大規模生産の論理に適合した道具で、高度に専門化されているので誰もが容易に使えるものではない。もう1つは、誰もが容易に使うことができるハンドツール（ハンマー、ノコギリ、電動工具など）。これらは各人の目的を達成するために使われ、自由の範囲を拡大し、生活の多様さをもたらす道具である。持つ者と持たざる者では使う道具が違う。土地も工場も生産機械も持たないドットアーキテクツでは、後者のハンドツールを武器にいろいろなものをつくっている。工業製品のような完成度は当然出ないが、それは問題ではない。そもそも工業製品には、つくる側と使う

側をはっきりと分けてしまう特性がある。大規模生産を前提としたものは、使い手個人の特異性があまり考慮されず、大多数が使い易いものにならざるをえない。それに比べてハンドツールでつくったものは、その場で修理もできるし、改造もできる。使い手が介入できる余地がそこにあり、個人の特異性に合わせて改変可能で、つくる側と使う側が不可分な状態をつくり出すことが可能になる。そういった考え方はプロダクトだけの話ではなく、さまざまな領域においても可能である。

私たちは「瀬戸内国際芸術祭2013」の「小豆島・醤の郷＋坂手港プロジェクト」の一環で香川県小豆島町の馬木地区に《UmakiCamp》という小さな集会所を建設した。当初は芸術祭の期間が終了すれば撤去だと聞いていた。場のあり方のお手本となったのは、2008年のG8北海道洞爺湖サミットの際に立ち上がった、マスメデ

ィアと違う視点で情報を発信する市民メディアセンターである。そこでは市民による情報の発信と共有が自発的に行われ、マスメディアからこぼれ落ちる情報を掬い取っていた。《UmakiCamp》でも、オルタナティブな公共空間を物理的につくり、地域の人々が自発的に関わり、既存施設ではバックアップできない町の活動を行っていけるような機会をつくり出したいと考えた。

　小豆島は瀬戸内海に浮かぶ島で、非架橋の島としては瀬戸内海最大であるが、人口減少と少子高齢化が最大の課題である。豊かな自然や風土、産業や福祉や教育をどう存続させていくかを考えると、誰かに頼るのではなく自主的に自分たちの状況をつくり出していくことが必要になる。もちろん集会所の建築そのものも構造家の満田衛資さんと一緒に考えて自分たちで建設できるものとした。コンクリートの基礎に空けられた穴に柱を差し込ん

で建てていく現代版掘立構造は、足場や仮囲い無しで脚立を使って１日で上棟させることができる。しかし建築という箱だけがいきなり建っても、誰もその使い方がわからなければ無用の長物となる。そこで建築と同時に地元の人同士や、地元の人と観光客を繋ぐメディアを用意した。そのなかのひとつに映画づくりがある。remo［NPO法人 記録と表現とメディアのための組織］が行っている「ご近所映画クラブ」という映画づくりワークショップのメソッドがある。ご近所や町内会などから集まったメンバーをグループ分けし、皆の話し合いで、脚本、配役、カメラ、小道具や衣装を決め、たった１日で映画をつくるというものである。そのワークショップを行いたいと馬木の方々に申し出たところ、皆が腑に落ちない顔をしていた。「われわれは凝り性だから、もっと前からきっちりと準備したい」、「グループに分かれてつくるのではなく、

皆で1本の映画をつくりたい」と言われ、ワークショップのメソッドを変更して、「それでいきましょう」と二つ返事で応答した。すると自治会館にある家具の引き出しから1冊の脚本が出てきた。それは映画『おくりびと』（滝田洋二郎監督、2008）をパロディーにした『思いやり』という演劇の脚本であった。この地域では敬老会のおりに演劇をする習慣がある。調べてみるとその歴史は古く、『資料集 総力戦と文化第1巻 大政翼賛会文化部と翼賛文化運動』（北河賢三編、大月書店、2000）のなかの「素人演劇を始めた動機」という項目で「小豆島安田村の演劇運動」が紹介されている。

あらゆる日本的な伝統は最もよく農村で保持され、又国力の基は農村にあり国力伸展の為めには農村の向上を計らなければならないと考へ、其為に最も必要な

ものは文化であり、然も之が農村で一番見捨てられて居ると痛感しますので、予てから此等の点を特に同志の間で考へ、同時に運動にも移してきました。

とある。安田は馬木とは別の地域であるが、馬木にも同様の状況があったのではないかと推測される。あんな時代、自由な言論や文化活動が消滅しつつあった時代に、最も必要なものは文化だと言える状況があったのかと感心した。また小豆島には肥土山と中山という地域に農村歌舞伎舞台があり、今でも年に1回地元住民によって大きな奉納歌舞伎が行われている。肥土山の農村歌舞伎を何度か見に行った。道路から階段を下り、神社の脇に出ると、神社の下に奥行き1・5m程度の芝の生えた客席が階段状に広がり、舞台に繋がっている。客席の脇には桟敷席があり、建物高さは低く抑えられ、欄干も低く良

いプロポーション。神社と桟敷席と舞台が地形に沿って客席を囲むように配置されていることで、空間に一体感をもたらしている。　皆が弁当を持って集まり、それはそれは素晴らしい状況である。《UmakiCamp》でもこの配置を活かし、道路に対して広場を全面的に開放するのではなく、道路沿いに山羊小屋を配置して視線を少し遮り、建物のメインボリュームと民家と寺の石垣で広場を囲むことで空間の一体感をつくっている。　農村歌舞伎は地区ごとの住民が毎年持ち回りで担当し、猛練習をして本番を迎える。　定番の演目の台詞には「昨日スナックで飲みすぎた」などタイムリーなネタが差し込まれて爆笑が起きる。　私の推測だが、地縁や血縁の強い小さな集落のなかでの日々の暮らしは、ときに閉塞感をもたらすがゆえ、自分ではない誰かを演じることのできる演劇や歌舞伎がある種のガス抜きの役割を果たしていたのではないだろ

うか。かつて農村歌舞伎がさかんに行われていた時代に、歌舞伎を楽しんでいた農民に対して役人が、楽しまずに働けということで歌舞伎を禁止しようとした際、農民たちが神様へ奉納しているのだと理由をつけて歌舞伎を存続させたとラジオで聞いたことがある。いつの時代も楽しみがないと生きている意味がない。

話を元に戻して映画の話であるが、『思いやり』という脚本は、葬式を題材にしているため敬老会で演じるには不向きということでお蔵入りになっていた幻の脚本であった。映画化が決まった数週間後には『瀬戸芸勝手に参加作品 喜劇 望郷編 思いやり』という映画の脚本に生まれ変わっていた。現在は人が亡くなると会館で葬儀を行うことが多くなっているが、かつては誰かが亡くなったときは、地域の人たち皆で協力して亡くなった人の家を葬儀の場へとつくり変え、家から故人を送り出していた。

この映画ではそうしたかつての葬儀がテーマになっている。部屋と部屋の間仕切りの襖を外すシーンが印象的だが、日本の家屋というのはこのように部屋が伸び縮みできて、使い方をいろいろと変化させられるのが良いところである。この映画にはシリアスなストーリーのなかに吉本新喜劇並みのベタなユーモアが織り交ぜられている。ビートたけしさんにも見ていただく機会があり、褒めていただくほどの映画が完成した。30人程度の配役はすべて地元の人たちに割り振られ、撮影日の午前9時にクランクイン、午後2時にクランクアップ、編集を経て夕刻から《UmakiCamp》の庭で映画上映会が始まった。地元の方々が多く足を運んでくださり、馬木の集落に笑い声が響いていた。私は葬儀屋Bという役をいただいた。建築も娯楽も誰かに与えられるのを待っていてはいけない。規模は小さくてもすべて自分たちで協力すれば、簡単な

道具によって状況をつくり出せるという実験をしたかった。建設中に仮囲いを設けなかったおかげで下校途中の小学生が端材で工作をしに来たり、近所の皆さんが差し入れを持ってちょくちょく遊びに来てくれた。植栽もしてくださった。この建築は最初から最後まで地域の方に見守られながら立ち上がった。そして《Umaki Camp》は公共の土地ではなく、前小豆島町長の塩田幸雄さん所有の土地に建っている。大昔からあったであろう地区の連帯と、町の援助、公と私が連携しながら誰もが使えるコモンスペースができあがった。塩田前町長は当時、自身のブログのなかで

一国で言うと、所管官庁のない、汎用型の新しいコンセ

プトの地域の拠点施設として、《UmakiCamp》で、福祉や教育、健康づくりなど、社会保障をはじめ、さまざまな課題を克服できる社会実験ができると思ったのです。

と述べている。《UmakiCamp》は瀬戸芸が終わっても小さな社会実験プロジェクトとして存続することが決まった。今でも馬木に建っているが、最近はあまり積極的に使用されていない様子であった。私たちは今でも馬木で別のプロジェクトに関わらせていただいていて、そのプロジェクトを推進している方が《UmakiCamp》を積極的に利用したいと申し出てくれている。《UmakiCamp》は建設から、映画づくりまで地元の方々や、地域団体である馬木ひしお会の皆さんにとてもお世話になった。

お好み焼き

私の友人で詩人の辺口芳典さんは、かつて父の収入がなくなったとき、母が突如お好み焼き屋さんをやることになったそうだ。商売はある程度繁盛してお客さんが付いていたが、次は母が体を悪くし、辺口さんがお好み焼き屋さんを継ぐことになった。最初は不慣れでお客さんにも迷惑をかけたものの、半年もすれば立派にお好み焼きを焼けるようになり、商売として成り立ったそうである。

私が勤める大学で職員をしている木原考晃さんは母子家庭に育ち、母親がパートタイマーとして働きながら木原さんとその姉を養っていた。木原さんが小学校3年生の時分に母親から「帰るのが遅くなってもいい?」と突然聞かれ、木原さんは母親が夜の商売に携わるのかとドキドキしたそうである。二十数年経った今もお好み焼き屋さんは繁盛し続け、立ち上げたときにいた同世代の4人のパートタイマーのおばちゃんたちも、誰ひとり辞めることなく今も一緒に働いている。私は関西で生まれ育ったが、昼ご飯で頻繁にお好み焼きが出てくるので食べ飽きていたこともあり、お好み焼きがそんなに好きではなかった。しかし、この話を聞いてお好み焼きをリスペクトせずにはいられない。お好み焼きは味が美味いだけでなく、生業にもしやすいところが素晴らしい。お好み焼きはまさに"鉄板"の食べ物なのである。

ベタとは何か。吉本新喜劇では何度同じギャグを聞いても面白い。それは、舞台上の役者の演技がとても生業にもしやすいところが素晴らしい。言い換えればベタである。ぽっと出の男前やきれいなだけの役者が軽く流したように演技しているのとは全然違い、基本がしっかりしているところに起因している。ぽっと出の男前やきれいなだけの役者が軽く流したように演技しているのとは全然違い、基本がしっかりしているのだ。

お好み焼きを分解して考えてみたい。素材は小麦粉、出汁、卵、キャベツ、揚げ玉など。あとはお好みの具材をベースにしている。これらの素材にプラスして各お店でアレンジが加えられる。どれも、どこでも手に入るもので目新しさはまったくない。道具は、まな板、包丁、ボウル、コテ、鉄板。扱うのが難しい道具は何ひとつない。スキルは、切る、混ぜる、焼く、裏返す。すごく簡単である。

素材、道具、スキルがシンプルで簡単でどこでも手に入るため、「いっちょやってみるか」となりやすい。お好み焼きの単価は比較的安いので多くの人がアクセスしやすい。そのことによって店ごとにさまざまな出来事が起こる。店によっては焼くのは客任せで、フィニッシュを預けてしまっているがゆえ、もはや誰がつくったのかわからない状態になっている。鉄板から直接食べることによってソースの焦げる匂いや音をダイレクトに感じ取り、温かいまま食べることができる。私がよく行くお好み焼き屋さんで、ある日隣で食べている年配のカップルが何やらゴソゴソしているので見ていると、カバンの中からカレー粉を出して、お好み焼きのネタの中にたっぷりカレー粉を入れて焼き出した。まったくメニューにない「カレーお好み焼き」の匂いが辺りに漂う。大胆なカスタマイズ。さらにお好み焼きには地域性もあり、関西のなかでも場所によって素材の配合や焼き方が異なる。

どこでも手に入る材料、誰もが扱える道具、簡単な技術、やりやすさ、出来事と地域性、基本を外さないカスタマイズ。お好み焼きは建築のメタファーになりえるのではないか。そしてドットアーキテクツが目指す建築のひとつはお好み焼きである。建築はさまざまな課題の合流地点であるが、その合流を鮮やかに見せてくれているお手本がお好み焼きである。

パニーニ

私が教員を務める大学の同僚、陶芸家の松井利夫さんに聞いた話である。1980年代にイタリアに留学していたとき、留学先の大学をサボって、いつも通っていたビリヤード屋さんの向かいにパニーニを売る屋台が出ていたそうだ。パニーニはひとつ500リラで売られていたらしいが、ある日パニーニをひとつ注文して1000リラ札を渡した。釣り銭を切らしていたパニーニ屋台のおっちゃんは、ためらうことなく札を半分にちぎり、半分になった札をつり銭として返してきたそうだ。それからしばらく経ってまたパニーニを買いに行った際に、手元に残った半分の札を渡すと、おっちゃんはそれを受け取り以前ちぎったもう半分の札とテープでつなぎ合わせて懐にしまったそうである。お金をちぎってはダメだと

思うのが普通の心情だが、お金を「1枚の価値のあるモノ」だと捉えるのではなく、単なる面積として捉えれば何当分でもできる。パニーニ屋のおっちゃんがなぜこんな気の利いたことができるのかと随分長い間考えていた。想像でしかないが、パニーニを手でちぎる癖が染み付いていたのではないだろうか。お金は抽象的な存在なので、そのモノ自体に置き換えなければならない。よくよく考えると結構まどろっこしいことができず、分けようと思えば別の価値のお金に置き換えることができる。たったひとつのパニーニが、世界を覆う貨幣システムのまどろっこしさを見せてくれた。モノや行為を一旦貨幣に置き換え、貨幣の量によって価値を計り、

ほかの多くのモノと交換可能になり、物理的な距離を超えることができる。貨幣は大した発明だと思うが、そのワンクッションがモノや行為と次に手に入るモノや行為との結びつきを希薄にしており、貨幣を手に入れる場所と使う場所が違うことによって、モノや行為の向こう側を想像する力を奪っているとも言える。

パニーニ屋さんのおっちゃんのお金の扱い方をヒントにさらに考えてみたい。お金は単体で持っていても何の役にも立たず、別のモノと交換するときに初めて意味が生まれる。つまり、「お金を使う」と言ったときの「使う」は、実際のところお金そのものを使っているのではない。お金そのものを使っている例で有名なのは、高級料亭の暗がりのなか、成金の老人が百円札を燃やし、灯にして靴を探している風刺画である。パニーニ屋さんのおっちゃんは、お金を交換するモノとして扱いながらも、それ自体を面積のあるモノとして捉え、半分にちぎると半分の価値のモノになると勝手に解釈している。抽象的な貨幣システムと、モノをちぎって分けるという具体的な行為が混じっていてややこしい。しかし、その具体

的な行為の差し込みに興味を惹かれる。抽象化することは人間の大発明であると思うが、一方で「モノ」と「使用」を分けてしまう。このことは私たちの暮らす大地に繋がっていく。

日本においては近世まで、土地は生産や居住など「使う」こととセットであり不可分であった。『土地と人間——現代土地問題への歴史的接近』(有志舎、2012)で丹羽邦男の文章が紹介されている。

近世の農民の土地所有は、具体的な、その土地の占有利用関係そのものである。すなわち、屋敷地に建てた住家に住み、自分のものである田畑を耕作し、用水・林野を利用するという具体的な、土地との関係(…中略…)が、近世の農民の土地所有であり、したがって、農民以外の身分のものは土地所有者になることはできない。

また、この性格は一定年数ごとに農民の耕作地をくじ引きによって割替える「割地制」に明瞭に現れると書かれている。土地は個人に「所有」されるものではなく、共同体で「使用」

されるものであった。しかし近代に取り込まれた一物一権主義の地租改正によって、土地が個人の所有物であることが法認され、自由に売り買いできるひとつのモノになってしまったので、使おうが使うまいが持つことができ、土地と使用が切り離された。現在、放棄された山林など所有者のわからない土地がたくさんあり、誰かが所有しているがまったく使われていない土地や家屋も多い。そのような土地が私たちの生存のために使われていないのはどういうことか。使われてない場所は解放し、町の小さな共同体によって使う場へ変えていくべきだ。1970年代にニューヨークのアーティスト、リズ・クリスティが荒廃した空き地に侵入してゲリラガーデニングを始め、近隣の人々のたまり場をつくった。この行為はガーデニングによって地域のコミュニティをつくったとも言えるが、"未使用"の土地を耕したところがミソである。未使用な公的建造物や工場を不法占拠して誰もが使える場に変えてしまうイタリアの「社会センター」も同様の事例である。私たちの多くは家賃やローン返済のために労働の対価とし

て得た金銭を場所に払い続ける。そのことが所有の意識を強めて共有の意識を追い出すことに繋がっており、土地をタダで使うことはたとえ空き地であっても許されないことになってしまっている。土地と使用をセットにし、かつそのセットの権利を多数の人で共有することを考えなければいけない。これを制度化すると多くの問題を孕むだろうから、パニーニ屋さんのおっちゃん程度に、軽い侵犯を通しながら、自らの工夫によっていい塩梅で一時的にでも状況をつくることができればいい。現在、土地に代表されるように、私たちを囲むさまざまなものへのアクセスは、最後の「使う」という行為や、サービスを「受け取る」という行為に閉じ込められる。資源に直接アクセスして、それらを組み立て、使うところまで、人やモノや環境に具体的に接触し、それらの合流点として、どのような建築をつくり出せるかを考えたい。

かつて大阪の河川敷に広がっていた畑の風景もいつの間にかなくなってしまった。しかし今でも、皆で耕す場を生み出して、皆で使う行為は、一部では存在していると思われる。

オン・ザ・ストリート

大正時代の浪曲家に添田唖蝉坊という人がいる。この人が書いた「乞はない乞食」(『浅草底流記』近代生活社、1930)というとても短い文章がある。ここでは路上でさまざまなパフォーマンスを行って生計を立てる人々が登場する。三味線を弾く指のない男や、相対性理論を自分たちの生活に引き寄せて面白おかしく演説する哲学者の乞食など。そしてその光景が、そこに登場する誰もが、底抜けに明るくていい。アニメ『じゃりン子チエ』にも路上のシーンが多く出てくるが、登場人物はとんでもない人が多い。主人公チエの父テツにいたっては、チエの同級生を平気でしばき回していた。今ではなかなかお目にかかれないような人間像もあり、そこには生き抜く術のバリエーションが示されている。

私は高校生の頃から現場作業員としてアルバイトをしていた。そこにチバさんというおっちゃんがいた。彼は水道屋さんであると同時に、ガス屋

さん、少しの大工仕事や土方、電気工事もしていたように記憶している。そしてすべて無免許だった。現場にはいつも軽自動車のバンでやってきたが、なんと車の免許すら持っていなかった。オールマイティに仕事をこなすが、腕は良いとは言えなかったのがまたいい。現在、職業と合わせて細分化された資格がどんどん生まれ、プロフェッショナルという単語に代表されるようにどこでも一流でなければ許されない風潮があり、ひとりの人間があれやこれやを生業にするのが難しい時代だ。この道一本で、ずっと会社勤めをやってきた人は定年退職を迎えた後、家で横になりながらドラマ『相棒』の再放送を見ることになる。閉じこもって家でテレビを見るより、路上で小さな商いでもして路上で活動が展開されるといいなと思う。クリーンになりすぎた街が失っている界隈性を取り戻せるかもしれない。

3年ほど前まで私は4階建集合住宅の3、4階

部分の小さなメゾネットに住んでいた。私の部屋の斜め下の2階に、ドレッドヘアーのいかついお兄さんが住んでいた。ある日、最終電車で帰り駅から家へ歩いていると、泥酔したドレッドヘアーのお兄さんが銀行の前のプランターに向かって吐いていた。酒を飲みすぎたのだろう。階段についた血痕がお兄さん部屋のドアまで続いていたこともある。素行はそんなに良いと思えなかったし、なんとなく敬遠していた。そんなある日、ベランダに干している私のお気に入りのシャツが風で飛ばされて、ドレッドヘアーのお兄さんの家のベランダに引っ掛かっているのが見えた。一瞬ためらったが、飛んでしまったシャツを取ってほしい旨をしたためた手紙にお菓子を添えて袋に入れ、ドレッドヘアーのお兄さんの家のドアノブに引っ掛けておいた。すると次の日、そのドアノブにシャツの入った袋が吊られていた。しかもシャツにはきっちりアイロンがあてられ、丁寧に折りたたまれていた。お礼をしたためた手紙にみかんとビールを添えて、またドアノブに引っ掛けておいた。それから洗濯物を干すときや洗濯物を取り入れるときに何気なくドレッドヘアーのお兄さんの家のベランダを見るようになった。そのベランダにはよくトラ猫がいた。だんだんそのお兄さんの印象が私のなかで変わりつつあったある日曜日、警察が3人私の部屋を訪ねてきた。「不審者を見なかったか?」との問いかけに、「見たことはない」と答えたのだが、ドアを開けてそっと状況を見ていると、どうやらドレッドヘアーのお兄さんが犯罪者をかくまっていたようである。窓からは捕まった人が警察に指差し確認させられている風景が見えた。程なくしてドレッドヘアーのお兄さんは、トラ猫をおいて引っ越していった。トラ猫はその集合住宅にしばらく居座り、2階のドレッドヘアーのお兄さんの部屋の向かいに住む青年が缶詰をあげているようだった。私もときどき、トラ猫に

オン・ザ・ストリート

ご飯をあげていた。しばらくして、そのトラ猫もどこかにいっていなくなってしまった。元気にしていればいいが。現在の集合住宅のあり方ではコミュニティが分断されるとか、一人暮らしの人同士のつながりをつくりづらいといった話を聞くが、面白いことが起きなくもない。しかし私が暮らした集合住宅で思い出すのはそのドレッドヘアーのお兄さんと向かいの部屋の女性が飼っていた太ったチワワの息遣いくらいである。この集合住宅に足りないものは路だったのだと気付くのは後のことである。

住んでいたメゾネットが手狭になってきたということもあり、土地や分譲マンションや賃貸の物件を5年くらい探してきたがしっくりくるものになかなか出会えない。集合住宅はどれも似た間取りと配列で、ただ部屋が広くなるだけでは何か新しい出来事に出会えそうもない。土地を買うことにも途中から抵抗感が出てきた。考えてみると今

まで自分の土地や自分の家を持ったことがない。生まれてからずっと借家に住んできたからか、地球の表面が切り売りされていることに違和感すら持つようになっていた。私自身が今は都心に住みたいので仕方ないが、地面をちょっとお借りします程度の気持ちがちょうどいいのではないかと考えている。間借りしているような、あちらとこちらがはっきりしないような、そんな場所を都市の中で見つけようとしていたのかもしれない。そんなことを考えていたとき、大阪の都心で古い路地と長屋に出会った。築106年、大阪大空襲で燃えなかった5軒長屋のうちの1軒。接道はしておらず、路地を2回曲がった先にある。道路から路地を見ると、突き当たりに錆びたトタンの長屋の側壁が見える。1回曲がると穴が3つ4つ空いたポリ塩化ビニルの波板が貼られた塀が見える。足元は薄いモルタルが剥がれてレンガが見えている。2回曲がると長屋の前の路地に出る。路地はきれ

いに掃除されていて、路地沿いに小さな菜園スペースがある。長屋の南側には住宅がぴったりとはり付いて建っているが、北側は公園で開けている。小さな公園のわりには銀杏、桜、クスなど大きな木が植えられていて季節感もある。長屋の中に入ってみると、畳は腐っていて、野良猫が住んでいる匂いがするが、構造は問題なさそうだった。1階はジトッとしていて暗いが、家人との話し合いの末、ようやくこの古い長屋に住むことに決めた。

オン・ザ・ストリート

このあたりは江戸時代に淀川の支流大川から引き込まれた堀の行き止まりで、壮絶なゴミの山ができていたそうだ。その後明治に入ってから大阪監獄ができる。当時はまだ市域の外側に位置していた場所である。日清戦争の前後から、大阪は紡績業を中心に商工業が発展し、市域が拡張され、人口が流入し、周辺の農村が都市化していく。この長屋が建ったのは、そういった急激な市街化によって場所の持つ意味や都市の空間的配置が大きく変化している時期にあたる。それから現在にいたるまで、大阪の中心部はつねに開発によってつくり変えられてきた。長屋は小さな島のように取り残されている。縦に積層された集合住宅は、見上げればタワーマンションが建っていて空は狭い。限られた土地に多くの人が住むことができる発明だとは思うが、地面から離れることで失うものも多い。現代芸術家の森村泰昌さん扮する町下路地蔵による『贋作「下町新党」党首演説』（2017）

から一部を抜粋する。

ともかく私の家の真ん前に立つ電信柱にですね、おしっこをひっかける犬がいるわけですよ。（…中略…）朝起きて外に出ると、黒く染みた尿の飛沫が、電柱付近に飛び散っている。これにホースで水をかけて洗い流すのが、私の日課となっております。

いつも、目線を足もとに落としておかないと、玄関先が臭くなる。日々、ていねいなお手入れを怠らぬ精神、これが下町に住むニンゲンの心意気であります。

（森村泰昌「下町物語プロジェクト」2017-2019、下町芸術祭2017 チラシより）

路地の菜園にせっせと水をやり、掃除している
と、ほかの長屋の住人といろいろと相談ができる
し、日々のちょっとした助け合いに繋がっていく。

路地は30cm先の小さな世界が続いて町になっているのだと教えてくれる。まわりには長く住んでいるじいちゃんやばあちゃんたちがいて、そのまた向こうに住んでいる人たちに連なっているのだとわかる。多くの住宅は家屋が車道に対して直接構えている。庭を挟んでいるとしても、その庭は私有地であり個人の家のバッファーにしかならない。家の前の道も、たまに通る車のために大きな空白地帯が家の前に広がっているに等しい。車道と家

が直接ドッキングしたような場は路上のさまざまな活動を誘発することができない。路地のような、そこで暮らしている人たちの共有のテリトリーでは、いつも小さな出来事が起こる。野良猫や知らないじいちゃんが網戸越しにこちらを見ている。

子どもたちは私の住む家を覗き込んで探偵事務所だと叫んでいる。秋には落ち葉で覆われていたり、お隣さんがパターゴルフをする音が聞こえてきたり、公園でかくれんぼをして家の前の植木に隠れている子どものケツが並んでいたりする。近所のおじさんがうちの菜園を勝手に横切って公園にアクセスする獣道のようなものをつくっているが、そのおじさんが「ネコちゃーん」と甘い声で野良猫を呼び餌をあげているのを見ると、まあいいかとなる。公園に勝手に植えたバナナに夜な夜なじょうろで水をあげていたが、強風で葉が折れてしまった次の日に、子どもを連れた母親が「バナナが折れちゃってるね」と子どもに話しかけているのが聞こえてきて嬉しい。この路地と長屋は、今までずっと都市の劇的な変化のなかにあった。今後10年の間に環境が大きく変わってしまうかもしれない。地面の上の、路地の暮らしは今後どう変わっていくのか。このどこにでもあった路地のような場所をどうすれば再び生み出せるのか。生きているものたちが織り成す予測不可能なものごとを共有しながら、前線で考えていきたい。

芝生の下

私が大学1回生のときのある夜中に、飼っていた犬が鳴き止まないのでおかしいと感じていた。その日の早朝、阪神・淡路大震災が発生した。ベッドから飛び起きたが、あまりの揺れに何もすることができず、一旦揺れがおさまってからまわりを見ると、土壁が落ち、物が散乱していた。電気はつかず、ガスも出ない。水は出るようだったので風呂場に水を貯めた。程なくして水も出なくなった。家の片付けをしていたときにラジオから「落ちてきたテレビがあたって怪我をしている人がいる」という情報が流れてきた。これが私の記憶している最初の怪我人の情報だった。少し時間が経つと被害の大きさがみるみる拡大していき、ついには阪神高速道路が横倒しになっているという。その近くに友達が何人か暮らしていたので、家を片付け、原付に乗って安否を確認しに行った。家のすぐ南に六甲山への登山口になる五叉路の交差点がある。当然信号機は壊れていたのだが、普段の交通量

も多いところだった。交差点の真ん中に立って車を手信号でさばいていたのは警察官ではなく、近所に住む一般のおじさんだった。原付で南に下るほど様相が一変していく。家は倒壊し、火事で燃え、道端には心臓マッサージをしている人がいる。とんでもない状況のなかを走り、友達が無事に避難所へ移動できているのを見届けた。中学校の同級生は瓦礫の中から人を救い出した後、倒壊した百貨店へ物資を取りに向かった。道路は歩道も車道もなくなっていた。インフラはシャットダウンし水も電気もガスも来ない。地域住民は皆、裏手の寺に湧く井戸水に並んだ。プロパンガスの風呂がある友達の家に、皆がお湯を借りに行った。米が炊ける人はおにぎりをつくって避難所に届けた。日頃のルールや善悪を超え、人々は協力しながら生き延びることを考えた。いろいろな問題や課題はあったにせよ、共同体とはこのように立ち上がるものかと考えさせられた。当時法学部に通っていた私は、ルールとは従うものではなく、自分たちでつくり出すものだと実感した。

私の生まれ育った家の近所には、山口組の本部があった。小学校の通学路にあった神社は山口組が法事の際などに使うので、そのたびに通学路が変わっていたと記憶しているが、とにかく日常生活のなかに当たり前のように山口組の存在があり、大きな屋敷が三角州に建っていた。まわりに住む人に危害が及ぶこともなく、ときには子どもの私にジュースを

買ってくれたり、声をかけたりしてくれていた。この辺りは治安のいい場所であったが、山口組は、警察ではないもうひとつの犯罪抑止力になっていたとすら思えてしまう。阪神・淡路大震災の際も、地域住民が食料不足で自衛隊の到着を待っているおり、自衛隊より早く地域住民にパンを配ったのが山口組だった。山口組の屋敷の前には長い行列ができ、地域住民は皆パンをもらった。私も袋を持ってその行列に並んだ。いかついお兄さんがパンを配ってくれていたが、持っていた袋を片手で差し出すと、「両手で袋を渡せ。お前は礼儀がなってないから、パンは1つじゃ」と言われた。この非常事態においても、礼儀を重んじるポリシーに沿って行動する態度に感心した。その屋敷の近くの川には「暴力団追放」と大きく書かれた看板が立っている。しかし、これはただ立っているだけで、地域住民は誰もそんなことを本気で考えていないのではないか。私は自分の街に、学校で習うこととはまったく違う原理で動く組織がいたことを、良かったとすら思っている。

芝生の下

カリブ出身の作家エドゥアール・グリッサンは、カリブ海のような多島の海を通して、さまざまな場所や状況が併存しながらネットワークを結んでいる状態を描いている。山口組が併存する街や、カリブ海の多島には、互いが関係しているようでしていないような状態で、調整を繰り返しながらぼちぼちと共存しているような均衡状態が見出せる。日々起きることや、その調整に時間を取られる煩わしさはあるが、同時に手を伸ばしたときに引っかかる突起がそこにある。ところがここ最近の私たちの生活の場は、突起を隠すようにきれいに張られた芝生の上に成り立っており、そうした均衡状態を失っていっているような気がする。

宮崎学による『近代ヤクザ肯定論──山口組の90年』（筑摩書房、2007）のあとがきには、近代のヤクザはNPOのようなものだったと書かれている。現行のシステムからこぼれ落ちるものを拾う役割があったということだ。阪神・淡路大震災が起こったのが1月。3月頃にまだ修繕されていない歩道を原付で走っていると、パトカーの拡声器から「もうあかんぞ〜」と聞こえてきた。「災害ユートピア」といった言葉もあるが、震災を通じて可視化されたさまざまな役割やルールは次第に消えていき、一部の地域では、かつてあった界隈性や近所付き合いを切断しながら、慌ただしい復興が進められていった。

空き地のかけら

私がかつて住んでいた借家と隣に建っていた家主の家の庭は広く、たくさんの樹木が生えていて小さな森のような雰囲気があった。庭には小さな祠まであり、毎朝家主がお参りしていた。私の母は、家主のおじいちゃんから、縁側の下で河童が火の玉を手の平で転がして遊ぶのを見た話を何度も聞かされたと言っていた。かつてはそのような生き物が身近に存在するという想像力をまだ持つことができたのだろう。どこもかしこも明るく照らされ、縁側のなくなった家のどこで河童は遊ぶのだろうか。室町時代に描かれたとされる絵巻物『付喪神絵巻』には、年末の煤払の日に捨てられた古い道具たちが付喪神となって人間を襲い享楽を尽くす話が描かれている。人間だけでなくモノにも得体の知れない蠢きを想像できる。

感性はとても大切だと思う。

明治以降、近代化のもとに政治や経済、地理が大きく変遷するなかで台頭した資本主義システムは、標準化して生産効率を上げることで低価格の商品を大量供給した。それによって労働者自体を消費の磁場にするという劇的な方法を発明した。製品の標準化が進むことで、差異というプレミアを纏った、狭い意味での〝デザイン〟が生まれた。そのようなモノたちから付喪神を想起するのは難しそうにも思える。

家主が亡くなった後、家主の親族が土地を売ったため、家と庭は潰された。次の建設工事が始まる前に、私の母が解体されて何もなくなってガランとした空き地に侵入し、草場の陰から5㎝角くらいの一欠片の陶器を拾って帰ってきた。そ

れは家族がまだ揃って暮らしていた頃、皆が毎朝顔を洗っていた洗面器のかけらだった。今、家族は別々に暮らし、亡くなった者もいる。たったひとかけらの小さなものになぜ心が動くのか。かつて京都文化博物館の地下を学芸員の村野正景さんに案内していただいたことがある。そこには、何百年、何千年の眠りを経てひょんなことから掘り起こされた数え切れない遺物たちが、ケースにしまわれて眠っていた。それらのかけらは、良いも悪いもなく、ただただかけらであり、過去に確かに生きていた名もなき人たちの営みの痕跡であり続けている。今このときも、地面の奥深くには、そっと眠っているたくさんのかけらがある。付喪神が消えた後でも、私たちの歴史はいろいろなところに小さく生きている。商品消費で満たされた世界を嘆いてばかりもいられない。取るに足らない小さなものにまで想像力を届かせたいものだ。

桜の噂

私が生まれ育った借家の前の道に1本の桜の木が生えていた。春にはいつもきれいな花が咲くので、家族で出かけるときや、小学校の学年が上がるときなど、節目節目にその桜の木の下で写真を撮った。私にとってもご近所さんにとっても、その桜は見慣れた風景であり、ずっとそこにあるものだった。

やがて借家の家主が亡くなり、その親族が土地を売ってお金に換えたいということで、家主の家も私が生まれ育った借家も取り壊されることとなった。現在はハウスメーカーがつくった味も素っ気もないプレハブの低層集合住宅が建っている。その集合住宅を建設する際に、邪魔になるという理由で桜の木を切ってしまう話が出た。道に生えているので切られてしまっても仕方がない。ところがご近所の方々はこの桜が咲くのを毎年楽しみにしていたので、工事の都合で切られることを良しとしなかった。そのようなおりに婦人会の集まりでひとりのおばちゃんが、この桜は天皇がこのあたりに来たときに愛でた由緒ある桜だと言い出したそうだ。皆もその話に乗っかり、桜の木は今も生えている。

もちろん根も葉もないでっち上げの話である。これは私が生まれるより前の話。家主が植木屋さんに桜の木を2

本持ってこさせた。そのうち1本を庭に植えたのだが、植木屋さんが余ったもう1本をどうするか尋ねたところ、家主が「道にでも植えといて」と言ったのが事の始まりだそうである。

『石山寺縁起絵巻』には良弁僧正が仏閣を建てようとして開拓した際に、土から大きな釣鐘が掘り出されたことを吉報だと言って社を建てて釣鐘を祀った話がある。掘ってたまたま出てきたものをありがたいものとしてこじつけ、事を進める推進力に変えている。物語の強さとは凄まじいものである。物語は本当であろうが、そうでなかろうが、ときに物事を動かす大きなエンジンとなる。

2013年の「瀬戸内国際芸術祭」で、ビートたけし氏とヤノベケンジ氏による、古井戸から起き上がる化け物の、最大6・5mまで伸びる可動式巨大彫刻作品《ANGER from the Bottom》が小豆島坂手地区に設置された。この彫刻作品は古井戸跡にあり、現在の自然と人間の関係に警鐘を鳴らすという意味が込められている。ビートたけし氏が来島した際には、彫刻作品を雨乞いや治水の神様として祀っていくために、町の方々によって「[水の神様]奉納祭」が行われ、神事が執り行われた。芸術祭の後、町の人々による、自然と作品を末永く大切にしていきたいという思いが高まった。自然を慈しみながら彫刻作品を風雨から守る社建設のために、小豆島町の自治会の代表、経済界、地元坂手の住民などで構成された「美井戸神社をつくる会」が発足し、小豆島の方々から集められた浄財によって美井戸神社のプロジェクトが進み出し、ドットアーキテクツで設計を担当することになった。このまるでフィクションのような話を見抜いた構造家の満田衛んなことが現実になるとは思ってもみなかった。

資さんは、さらなる過激なアイデアを構造設計で練っていく。伸び縮みする彫刻作品に合わせて社も伸び縮みさせようというもので、基礎をシリンダーとして扱うことによって社自体の昇降を可能にしている。彫刻作品を動かさない時期は屋根を低く抑え、背後にせまる洞雲山の景を邪魔しないように配慮し、彫刻作品を動かす時期は社自体を持ち上げる。曳家ではなく、伸家である。そして「美井戸神社をつくる会」は、竣工後には「美井戸神社を守る会」へと名称が変更された。

設計行為にはいつも冷静な判断が求められる。建物の目的や使用者の要望、法規、コストや物理的な問題など、そこにある事実を統合して答えを導いていく。物語があろうがなかろうが、建築は自律したものであり、良い建築は良いと言ってしまえばそれまでで、そこに物語は必要ない。しかし、降って湧いたようなことでも取り込む包容力をもって、釣鐘のように、そこにあった物語をもその建築が存在していることの理解に繋げたい。文化人類学者の小川さやかさんが言っていた。「噂話は最も原始的なメディア」であると。

数年前、大阪の北加賀屋にある事務所の前の公園で83歳（本当かどうか怪しい）のおじいちゃんと話し込んだ。徳島県の山間に生まれ、小さい頃に母親を亡くし、兄弟全員散り散りに徳島県の山から出ていったそうだ。子どもの頃は雪の降る日も裸足なので見様見真似でわらじをつくり、竹でスキー板をつくって山中を移動した。当時は父子家庭になっても国からの援助なんてなかったから今は良い時代だ、明石海峡大橋ができて車で海を越えられるなんて漫画みたいだ、高速道路を走って遠いところまですぐに行けるなんて夢のようだ、労働基準法ができて労働者の環境が嘘みたいに良くなった、自転車が気軽に買えるなんて幸せだ、と言っていた。糖尿病になり心臓のバイパス手術をして、胃癌と大腸癌と肝臓癌になり、緑内障と白内障になったけれど、子どもの頃のタフな生活があったから元気なんだと笑っていた。仕事もいろいろし てきた。奈良の集落がひとつもない山奥で木を伐採して山を越えて運搬する仕事をしたり、自衛隊ではバズーカ砲や迫撃砲を打ち、鉄工所でも働いていたそうだ。ついこの前まではゲートボールの審判をしていたが責任を伴うから辞めた、歌

が好きだからいつも歌っていると言っていた。あまりに話が面白く、事務所に帰ってすぐに書き起こしをした。この立ち話のなかには福祉、医療、高齢化、仕事、近所付き合いなど、大切なことが多く詰まっているし、かつての欠乏や問題がさまざまな努力によって解消されてきたこともわかる。おじいちゃんが言う「夢の時代」が到来して世界は広がったとも言えるが、次から次へと新しい問題が生まれている。

私の知り合いが、独居老人の住む家の改修工事を受注した。工事中の間、家には住めないので、数日間別の場所で寝泊まりしてもらったそうだが、そのたった数日間にご老人は認知症を発症したらしい。ご老人にとっては、長く住む自分の家が世界のすべてになっていたのではないだろうか。あそこの魚屋さんに行けばあのおっちゃんがいる、私が繕った服をあの子が着ている、あそこの植木は私が手入れしたなど、町の中に自分のテリトリーを広げておくことができれば認知症の状況が変わったかもしれないし、認知症になったとしても施設に閉じ込めずに町に開かれた状況で暮らすことができるか

もしれない。他者との関係と合わせて、星座のように描かれた場所との関係が大切ではないか。そのテリトリーをつくることができるかどうかが私たちの住む町や村の未来を左右すると思われる。

私たちはアート、オルタナティブ・メディア、アーカイブ、建築、地域研究、サークル、NPO、デザイン、FabLab、木工など分野にとらわれない人々や組織が集まる協働スタジオとして、元家具工場の廃屋を改修した「コーポ北加賀屋」を拠点に7つのチームで延べ床面積750㎡の場所をシェアしている。それぞれのチームの部屋と別に作業スペースやイベントスペースとして使える150㎡の場所が2つある。コーポ北加賀屋のある大阪市住之江区北加賀屋という場所はかつて造船業でたいへん栄えた場所であり、近代大阪の繁栄を支えてきたが、産業構造の変化によって工場が移転、減少し活気が失われつつある。当時は何万人という造船業に関わる人たちが暮らしており、同じ町内に喫茶店が5つあったほどであるが、造船所が移転した後、空き家や空き地が増え、町内に

してしか想定されていない物件は、ものづくりを生業にして
いる人やアーティストのアトリエにはたいへん使いにくい。
アーティストやデザイナーにとって安い家賃や原状回復なし
といった好条件によって、今では少しずつ賑わいを見せ、2
009年には「北加賀屋クリエイティブビレッジ構想」が立
ち上がり、点々と存在していたアトリエを線で結び連携して
いくことが試みられている。

そのような空き家のなかに「千鳥文化住宅」というものが
あった。1階は喫茶店や散髪屋などの商店として使われ、2
階は「文化」という名前がついてはいるが、迷路のように小
さな部屋が連なる当時の労働者の住まいとして使われていた、
2階建て下駄履き住宅である。築年数も相当なもので、千鳥
文化住宅の1階にお店を構えていた当時を知る喫茶店のママ
に聞き取りをしてみると、造船所が賑わいを見せていた頃は
多くの外国人も短期滞在していたそうで、店先に干していた
雑巾は風呂屋の手ぬぐいとして勝手に持って行かれたり、洗
濯機も外に置いているとすぐなくなるのでチェーンで固定し

あった最後の喫茶店も数年前に閉店となった。そういった場
所の多くを所有する千島土地株式会社は、土地や建物の賃貸
を生業としているわけだが、借り手が転居したり亡くなった
りした後に上家付きで返却された土地は、住宅の耐用年数や
メンテナンス費の問題などからもう一度誰かに貸すには競争力
を持たないため、空き家や空き地を手っ取り早くコインパー
キングに変えてきた。しかし、コインパーキングだらけの町は
魅力を失っていく一方なので、2003年より造船所跡地を
アートの実験場(現クリエイティブセンター大阪)として活用した
り、鋼材加工工場および倉庫跡の大きなスペースをアーテ
ィストの巨大彫刻作品収蔵庫「MASK MEGA ART STORAGE
KITAKAGAYA」とし、年1回は開放して地域内外の方々に
アートを体感してもらう場として活用したりしている。また
小さな空き家や空き地の活用法として、アーティストやデザ
イナーに原状回復をしないでいいという条件で賃貸物件とし
て貸し出した。私たちが通常賃貸物件を借りると、退去時の
原状回復のために壁に釘を打つのもためらわれるし、いつま
でもその場所との関係がよそよそしいものに感じる。住居と

ていたりしたそうだ。火事も多く、「また加賀屋が燃えている」とよく言ったらしく、たいそう賑やか（物騒）だったそうだ。今でも、知り合いが車を停めている間に窓ガラスを割られて車の中から工具をきれいさっぱり盗まれたことがある。多分どこかで売られているだろう。千鳥文化住宅の建物自体は、一説では船から出てくる材料や解体現場から出てきた資材を使って船大工が建てたらしく、鴨居や柱が梁や壁の下地材として利用されており、今にも朽ちそうな趣であるが、最後まで暮らしていた92歳の独居老人が家族に引き取られたことで完全に空き物件になったことから、この場所を活用していく話が持ちあがった。「千鳥文化」と名前を変え、千島土地株式会社、graf（ディレクター）、ドットアーキテクツ（設計・運営）、小西小多郎（運営）の4者協働で運営をスタートし、現在もメンバーで運営や企画などいろいろと試行錯誤しながら進行中である。

千鳥文化は私たちの事務所から歩いて3分。私たちは北加賀屋で活動してはいたものの、実際にまわりの工場の人や地域住民と関わる機会は皆無であった。そろそろ町の中に新し

い手触りのある場所をつくり出し、地域で暮らす人と働く人が緩やかに交流する時間と場所を生み出すことで、北加賀屋でのテリトリー形成を試みようとしている。テリトリーと言っても強い縄張り意識ではなく、私が居てもいいんだと思える家以外の場所のことを指している。そのためにさまざまな機能が入り混じった計画をしている。1階には、食堂、バー、商店、アトリウム（誰もが入れる場所でイベントやライブラリーとしても使われる）があり、2階にはおおさか創造千島財団が運営する小さなギャラリー（通称：部屋プロジェクト）が6部屋ある。建物の裏にはNPO法人 Co.to.hana の運営する市民農園があり、つい最近にはB棟と呼んでいる手付かずのまま放置していたスペースの改修が終わり、大きめのギャラリースペースとテナント区画ができた。その9つのテナントではアーティストのアトリエや市民農園の方々の惣菜屋さん、ヨガ教室などがすでに稼働している。千鳥文化食堂は、地域に開きつつ、コーポ北加賀屋や周辺で働く人たちの社食のような役割を持っており、バーはドットアーキテクツの家成、土井亘、寺田英史と contact Gonzo の三ヶ尻敬吾さんと一緒に運営していて、

ときどきゲストバーテンダーで建築家やデザイナーやアーティストに立ってもらっている。お客さんはほぼご近所の方々で、いつもいろいろな話ができてとても楽しい。また、すでに海外では古材バンクが機能し、ホームセンターのような大きさのスペースで古材の売買が行われているが、北加賀屋でも依然として解体される物件が多く古い建具や金物などが出てくるため、それらを捨てずにもう一度アトリエや住宅の改修材料として活用し資材の地域内循環をつくれるよう、千鳥文化の1階に古材バンクをオープンした。なかなか売れずに苦戦し、今ではアーティストのアイテムや三ヶ尻さんが海外公演の際に買い付けた面白いものも合わせて販売している。

設計だけでなく自ら運営にも関わることで、いろいろな人に出会えるし、常連さんのテリトリーのようなものもできあがるし、たまたま来た来訪者との出会いの場も増える。

設計だけでなくバーテンダーもやるといったように、いくつかの役割を自分の働く場所で持つのがいい。千鳥文化は今後、運営しながらさまざまにカタチを変えていくことが予想されるが、農園、食、バー、商店、ライブラリー、イベント、アートなど、決めきらずにさまざまな人たちと連携しながら実験をしていきたいと考えている。そして何より自分が楽しみたい。

私は千鳥文化の運営に関わっていて、月に1、2回ほどバーテンダーとして店に立っている。建築家がバーテンダーを設計と同時にやるのは、どこか不真面目な印象を持たれるかもしれない。現在、千鳥文化の食堂をまわしているのは映像エンジニアの小西小多郎さんとアーティストの望月梨絵さん、元劇団維新派の役者で劇団のまかない飯をずっとつくっていた石本由美さんで、商店はcontact Gonzoの三ヶ尻敬吾さんが切り盛りしている。いろいろな人が各自の持つ専門性を超えて運営に関わっている。

かつて粘菌を事務所で育てていたことがあるが、

粘菌は現在の環境に生き方すべてを合わせていくことがないそうだ。つねに何パーセントかは役に立たず、遊んでいる状態だと、北海道大学教授で粘菌の研究者である中垣俊之さんや大阪大学教授の上田昌宏さんから教えていただいた。その理由は、環境が激変した際に、大半が機能しなくなっても、残りの遊んでいるかのような別の体が次の環境に合わせて生き延びることができるからだ。かといって私たちは設計を生業とすることが厳しくなったときのためにバーテンダーをやっているわけではない。設計に閉じず職種を跨ぐように嬰わりを広げることで、地域に接する機会を増やし、そ

こで起こるいろいろなことを建築に活かしていきたいと考えている。『南方熊楠全集 別巻 第一』（平凡社、1974）のなかに次の文章がある。

Comatricha nigra と *C. laxa, Trichia affinis* と *T. persimilis* と *T. favoginea* と *T. scabra, Stemonitis herbatica* と他の数種などときては、判然たる本種とすべきものは少なく、どちら付かずの中間物ははなはだ多く、また *Stemonitis fusca; St. splendens; St. ferruginea* 等の内には本種とすべきか変種とすべきか異態とすべきか去就に迷うものはなはだ多く、変種同志の間にまた無数の中間変種あり。故に多く見れば見るほど、天地間にこれが特に種なりと極印を打ったような品は一つもなく、自然界に、属の種のといういうことは全くなき物と悟るが学問の要諦に候。

（アルファベット表記はすべて菌類の学術名称）

熊楠さんは、菌類を分類してまとめて考えるこ

とより、その一つひとつの存在に着目すべきだと言っている。バーに立っていると、「地域の人」ではなく「〜さん」や「〜くん」といった個性に出会っていく。今福龍太さんのジョン・ケージのお話を聞いたことがある。『ジョン・ケージ――小鳥たちのために』を引用しつつ、

「ストーニーポイントはあらゆるキノコの宝庫です。キノコを知れば知るほどそれを識別する自信が薄れていくのです。一本一本が違っていますから。それぞれのキノコがそれ本来のものであり、自らの中心にあるのです。キノコに詳しいなどということは無駄なことです。キノコは人間の知識を裏切りますから。」

と仰っていた。ジョン・ケージは辞書で music の1つ上に mushroom があったことからキノコに興味を持ったらしい。その後、ニューヨーク菌類学

会の創立に関わり、キノコ研究者としても知られている。ジョン・ケージの偶然性や即興性の背後にはキノコが生えている。

ドットアーキテクツは設計のほかにかなりの数の施工や制作に関わる仕事をしてきた。そして事務所のメンバーだけでやるのではなく、気の合う

仲間たちと一緒に取り組んでいくことが多い。いい加減現場に出るのをやめろとよく言われたものだが、現場であれやこれやと思案し、より面白いと思う方向へと体を動かしてつくることそのものに歓びを感じている。一回つくってみて壊すこともある。何と非効率的なと思うかもしれないが、それが楽しいのだから仕方ない。一種の蕩尽とでも言える貨幣の価値に置き換えることができないものに、思考と体を注ぎ込んでいく。一回こっきりの現場のノリやグルーヴやムラを楽しみ、それによってできあがるもののために調整を繰り返したり、即興ですぐかたちにすることもある。私たちも一緒に仕事をする仲間も、現場が始まる前にフリスビーやキャッチボールで遊ぶ。そしてそのまま地続きに、フリスビーをしているように現場作業をする。いっそ仕事と遊びを分けず、すべてを遊び化して建築に向かっていきたい。自ら路上商人となりながら、タンザニアの路上商人を研究

している文化人類学者の小川さやかさんに聞いたお話だが、路上商人たちは、系統立った組織を持たず、各々が利己的に振る舞いながら、ギリギリのところで他者への配慮を持っているという。一応組合のようなものがあるが、その組合も「シティバスの路線図のようなもの」らしく、誰でも、いつでも、どこからでも乗り込み、いつでも降りることができるらしい。新陳代謝をそれぞれの判断で繰り返し、組織として捕まえようのない状態は、方向転換や、生き方をその場その場で変化していくことができる。きっちりとした合議制というより、場当たり的な調整を繰り返しグニャグニャとやっていくスタイルは面白いなと思う。ドッ

トアーキテクツは小さな組織ではあるが、できるだけシティバス感をつくりたいものだ。半ば強制的に全員で毎日会議を行い、一日の作業内容の報告を行った際には、事務所全員のテンションがみるみる下がって顔色が悪くなっていった。ドットアーキテクツはそういうメンバーばかりである。

事務所のスタイルやブランディングなどの固定化を免れ、変幻自在にその場その場でやり方を変えて、粘菌のように、路上商人のように、すべての可能性に開かれた状況を、建築を通してつくっていきたい。なのでカウンターの中でお酒をつくっていることも、また良しだし、一杯のジントニックも建築と言えるのだ。

パーティー

今から20年ほど前、神戸にあるクラブで行われたパーティーの内装がドットアーキテクツのキャリアのスタートである。たった一晩のために鉄筋を2tほど地下のクラブに運び込み、2日間そこで寝泊まりしながら結束線で巨大な籠のようなものを組み上げて空間をつくり、そのままパーティーに突入した。次の日の朝には鉄筋をバラして撤収して、元の箱に戻した。後日、これをさらに発展させるカタチで行った3日間連続のパーティーでは、木材を持ち込み、夜はパーティー、昼はその木材を組み替えて毎晩違う空間を出現させ、3日間ほとんど寝ずに場所を変化させ続けた。そしてまたすぐバラして元の箱に戻した。2017年秋に行われた「港都KOBE芸術祭」では、神戸大橋という本州と人工島ポートアイランドを結ぶ巨大な橋の下に、仮設の野外クラブ「UNDER THE BRIDGE」を期間限定でオープンした。神戸で小さなライブスペース兼ギャラリースペースを営む友人や、神戸にゆかりのあ

るDJの方々に登場してもらい、1カ月間、毎週末、秋の港に夜まで音が鳴り響き、ゆっくり音楽を聞く人から我を忘れて踊る人まで、さまざまな人に楽しんでもらえたと思う。

DJやミュージシャンも入れ替わり、来るお客さんもさまざまに動き、空間も変容しながらすべてが動的な状態のなかでパーティーが進んでいく。最後にはきれいさっぱりなくなるその一時的空間は、そういった偶然性やノリや即興を取り込み、高揚感や、いろいろな居場所をつくっていくことができる。

『T.A.Z.——一時的自律ゾーン、存在論的アナーキー、詩的テロリズム』（箕輪裕訳、インパクト出版会、2019）のなかでハキム・ベイは、S・パール・アンドリューズの『ザ・サイエンス・オブ・ソサエティ』を引用しながら、

ディナー・パーティーのように数人に門戸を開いているか、あるいはビー・インのように何千人もの参加者に開放しているかを問わず、「指図されていない」ためにパーティーは常に「開かれて」いるのであって、それは計画されたものかもしれないが、もしも〈偶発する〉ことがなかったならば、それは失敗なのだ。自発性の要素は、大変に重要なものである。

パーティーの本質はつまり、面と向かって、人間の集団が相互の欲望を実現しようとする彼らの努力を補佐することにある——それがおいしい食べ物や乾杯、ダンス、おしゃべり、生活の技術のためのものであっても、おそらくはエロティックな快楽を求めてのものでさえあっても、あるいはコミューン的アートワークを創造するため、または至福の忘我を達成するためのものであっても——（…中略…）または、クロポトキンの用語で言えば「相互扶助」への基本的な生物学的動機である。

と述べている。現代を生きる私たちはこういった意味でのパーティーの機会をますます失っている。集まるのはカラオケボックスや居酒屋になり、ある特定の目的が中心にあり、かつそれらの場所を、お金を払って手に入れている。ここで言うパーティーとは、集まる人たち（2人でも大人数でも）の目的はバラバラでもよく、居場所を見つけることができるものであり、現行の社会のなかにおける役割とは別の立ち振る舞いがある。ゴールもない。そこでは日に日に、時間ごとに、関係性が入れ替わり、いろいろな自分が許容される。私たちが社会の課題を捉えて建築で応えようとする際に、その解決策を見つけ、再びその社会のなかで機能するようにしたとしても、そもそもその社会は課題を抱えていた社会であり、

そこに引き戻すことでしかない場合が多々ある。パーティーのような一時的に立ち上がるオルタナティブな空間が、日常で課せられた役割を反故にし、いろいろな意味で違う接触を促し、生き方のバリエーションを与えてくれる。パーティーができるかどうかが良い建築かどうかのひとつの指標ではないかと最近考えている。既存のディスコミュージックから溢れる音を仲間たちと家で楽しんだことから「ハウス」と名付けられたと言われる音楽のジャンルがあるように、何も家の外だけにパーティー空間があるのではない。住宅も含め、そこでパーティーをすることをイメージしながら設計をしていきたい。

クォーターバックが運転するピックアップトラックの荷台に乗って、親の居ぬ間にパーティーをやっている家に乗り付け、チェストの上においてあるツボにゲロを吐くという友人から聞いた映画のようなお話。それもまた良しである。

Contemporary Architect's Concept Series 27

dot architects | Cut Trees on the Mountain,
Make a Boat, Float It on the Sea

LIXIL Publishing

プロジェクト

p. 100　サーチプロジェクトvol.4「ニュー“コロニー／アイランド”〜“島”のアート&サイエンスとその気配〜」
プロジェクトメンバー：
上田昌宏（大阪大学理学研究科教授）、中垣俊之（北海道大学電子科学研究所教授）、
ドットアーキテクツ（建築家ユニット）、yang02（アーティスト）、稲福孝信（アーティスト、プログラマー）
©アートエリアB1、2015、photo by Nobutada Omote

p. 102　鉄道芸術祭vol.5 クロージングイベント「これからの、もうひとつの電車」
監修：ホンマタカシ
出演：NAZE、小山友也、PUGMENT、ドットアーキテクツ、三重野龍、contact Gonzo
©アートエリアB1、2015、photo by Yoshikazu Inoue

写真

西光祐輔　　表紙
JP/ p. 9–24、31、34、40、41、47、52、56、57、60、61、67、70、72、73、76、83、89
EN/ p. 9–24、26、28、31、32、35、38、40、42、45、47、48、50、54、56

松見拓也　　p. 101　contact Gonzo「ゴンゾ解體新書（かいたいしんしょ）」13分間東屋
濱田英明　　p. 104　UmakiCamp
井上嘉和　　p. 101　KYOTO EXPERIMENT 2017 神里雄大／岡崎藝術座《バルパライソの長い坂をくだる話》
　　　　　　p. 102　鉄道芸術祭vol.5 クロージングイベント「これからの、もうひとつの電車」
表恒匡　　　p. 100　サーチプロジェクトvol.4
　　　　　　「ニュー“コロニー／アイランド”〜“島”のアート&サイエンスとその気配〜」
ドットアーキテクツ　　上記以外

現代建築家コンセプト・シリーズ27
ドットアーキテクツ｜山で木を切り舟にして海に乗る

発　行　日　　2020年10月1日　第1刷発行
著　　　者　　家成俊勝
発　行　者　　ジン・ソン・モンテサーノ
発　行　所　　LIXIL出版
　　　　　　　〒136-8535 東京都江東区大島2-1-1
　　　　　　　TEL. 03-3638-8021　FAX. 03-3638-8022
　　　　　　　http://livingculture.lixil.com/publish/

企画・編集　　中村睦美、飯尾次郎（スペルプラーツ）
翻　　　訳　　アラン・グリースン
デ ザ イ ン　　浅田農（MATCH and Company Co., Ltd.）
印　　　刷　　株式会社加藤文明社

ISBN978-4-86480-048-8 C0352
©2020 by dot architects. Printed in Japan

乱丁・落丁本はLIXIL出版までお送りください。
送料負担にてお取替えいたします。

● Contents

Preface

Toshikatsu Ienari (co-director, dot architects)

Our daily lives are surrounded by flux. Among the myriad things laid out around us, some change gradually on a time scale measured in centuries, while others change from season to season, and still others from day to day. They range from mountains, rivers, expressways and railroads to our house, our kitchen table, the cookie crumbs scattered across the tabletop—and from things thoroughly planned out to those occurring on a whim. We also participate in all kinds of groups—households, schools, workplaces, neighborhood associations, online communities—with varying degrees of intensity. People may move, or stay in one place; their ideas may change over time, or they may not. Arrangements and relationships constantly in flux: this is the immutable condition under which we live. Architectural design typically takes its cues from things that do not readily fluctuate, but I prefer to imagine another approach that allows us to respond to dynamic conditions, to the new things that arise every day—things that exist and things we desire in the here and now.

We have grown accustomed to our position as recipients of services provided by the national or local government. This has the effect of alienating us from the act of creating our own spaces ourselves. At the same time, we are increasingly surrounded by things of such complexity that only so-called specialists can figure them out—Japan's recent "legislation explosion" of new laws being a case in point. So we find ourselves consigned to the receiving end of conditions that we assume, from the outset, we can't

possibly understand. But systems and spaces do not descend on us like rain from above; they grow out of the ground. We live on the ground, and our respective bits of ground are connected, forming the collective ground upon which we carry out our daily lives.

One characteristic of the work of dot architects is the diversity of our interests, which extend beyond conventional architectural design to such undertakings as construction, event planning, art projects, performances, and venue management. We work on structures that are meant to stand a long time but also some that stand for a while, then are torn down, and some that last only twenty minutes. Works of any type or lifespan will eventually disappear, so why not treat all of them as temporary structures? This doesn't mean simply rejecting the usual reams of forecast data or future scenarios while extolling the autonomy of architecture, but rather responding to the here and now with the flexibility to modify one's strategies like a surfer riding the waves. Instead of employing surveys and marketing campaigns to draw a line between creator and consumer—and treating consumers as all of a kind—I would like to pursue a different approach: focusing on a specific set of circumstances, riding the waves that well up there, ignoring what anyone says is socially correct, and looking for areas of compromise with idiosyncrasy and perversity.

In his book *Psico-Nautica: Anthropology of Italian Psychiatry* (Sekaishisosha, 2014), Associate Professor Takeshi Matsushima of the Graduate School

of Social Sciences, Hiroshima University discusses the movement to abolish mental hospitals in Italy. That movement used the slogan "Da vicino nessuno è normale" (Up close nobody is normal). What is normal? What is correct? I think such notions are found, not in the aggregate of invisible forces we call society, but in the conflicts among diverse lines of reasoning that arise from the diverse conditions in which we live.

Let me introduce the words of Mr. Shin Harada as quoted by Kohei Inose in his book *Village and Nuclear Power Generation: Shimanto People Who Covered Up the Construction Plan of Kubokawa Nuclear Energy Plant* (Rural Culture Association, 2015):

> After many "pointless" meetings and "pointless" arguments, we reach a "there, there" kind of compromise. Some people may think it would make more sense to present a good arrangement from the start, but that means they don't know how a village works. For a village, compromise can happen only after an argument. Or rather, our arguments never go on forever because if we argue, it will always produce wisdom leading to compromise. The way the word "compromise" gets used these days, maybe it's better to call this "deferring to each other." [. . .] Giving up and accepting. It's a "well, it can't be helped" kind of acceptance. City people aren't likely to understand this. It's not the same as "okay, whatever." It's because if we didn't give up, we wouldn't be able to go on living in the

same village together. No one wants that. Is it wrong to call this a kind of wisdom?

When I first began studying architecture, I was told over and over not to use the pronoun "I" in my design presentations. They admonished me that phrases like "what I like" or "what I think" make it sound like "my world" is a narrow closed one that cannot be shared by others and that I'm arrogant enough to believe that I can design architecture entirely on my own. And yet, most of the topics I address in this book begin with my personal experiences, trivial but outside-the-box events. In relating these little occurrences as the personal experiences they were, I'm trying to be anything but closed. Rather, I'm hoping that they might offer us some hints for creating original spaces that transcend the prearranged spaces around us. Not all my stories of things I've seen and heard have a coherent plot, but by interpreting those plotless narratives as we like and coming up with ideas that make sense of them, we may find ways to link my world with your world and, through our collective imaginations, turn those ideas into physical spaces. The multifarious occurrences in our daily lives give rise to elusive sensations and emotions, improvisations, inspirations and pleasures. There we can find hints for dealing with architecture, for unearthing hidden uses for a given place, for expanding the scope of possibilities. The very fact that we exist flush with the ground—that, above all, is what I find fascinating.

Rokko Housing

I was born and raised at the foot of Mt. Rokko in Hyogo Prefecture. The mountain behind my house was my childhood playground. When school was out my friends and I would head for the mountain, climbing barely traceable paths and tumbling down slopes covered with dry leaves. We built several primitive huts in the forest from the fallen trees and branches lying there. We were the proprietors of our very own rustic teahouses, and the mountain was our garden. This was the mountain where Rokko Housing I, designed by Tadao Ando, stood. We were told that a famous architect had created it. Even we kids could see that this concrete complex built flush against the hillside was different from other buildings in the area. At the time I lacked the aesthetic sensibility to judge if it looked good or bad, or the imagination to think about the challenges faced by the designer and builders. I just remember the impression that some sort of weird alien fortress was standing there in the middle of nowhere.

One day we found that our mountain had been clear-cut and our funky huts hauled away. Construction of Rokko Housing II had begun. Every day I gazed bitterly at the hillside where we had been deprived of our playground. But by the time I entered middle school I was no longer interested in playing in the woods, and after a while Rokko Housing III appeared.

At some point the house next door to ours was torn down and replaced by a parking lot. With the view from the little toilet window now unobstructed, I could see Rokko Housing through the screen whenever I took a leak. In hindsight, this may have been where my interest in architecture began.

In high school I took a part-time job at a construction company where the father of a boyhood friend worked. My tasks included walking around building sites picking up trash, hauling materials, and helping pour concrete or tear things down. In college I worked part-time as a rebar placer for a company run by the husband of a middle-school classmate. While lugging rebar for grade beams in the midsummer heat, covered with mud and sweat, all I could think about was the money I was making each day. Rokko Housing was just a buried memory, and I came to view architecture purely in terms of construction sites. Just as graduation day was approaching and I was searching for full-time work, Japan's economic bubble collapsed. I had been thinking that rather than be a company employee, I'd prefer to work on my own making something or other. But instead of pursuing this goal I spent my time getting drunk in a Kobe bar. The bartenders there all had distinctive personalities, and information about liquor, music, and fashion flowed back and forth. In the tiny space around the 50-centimeter-wide counter you could find fishermen, company presidents, Hanshin Tigers fans—all manner of utterly unrelated people sitting side by side, engaging in chat ranging from high culture

to rumors to small talk of every sort. The information exchanged was diverse and entertaining. One of the bartenders had studied architecture in college, and one day he asked me, "You know anything about architecture?" Since I had done construction work for years, I replied that I certainly did. He thereupon handed me a book by Arata Isozaki and Akira Asada, *Anywhere—Problems of Space* (NTT Publishing, 1994). I took it home and began reading it, but found that I couldn't understand a word. I had no idea what sorts of "problems" it was talking about. For someone whose book reading was limited to the occasional novel, this was a jarring experience that triggered my interest in the vast world of architecture and brought me back to Tadao Ando. I decided to become an architect myself and began attending a technical college at night while working as a bartender. I also began making frequent visits to Rokko Housing. I would sit on the stairs midway up the slope and look out into the distance past the beams that extended over my head toward the sea. I bought and devoured a book of Ando's architectural details, which included a section on Rokko Housing. In a large pullback shot of the area around the complex, the tile-roofed house right in front of it with the laundry hanging out to dry is the house I was born and grew up in. It's no longer there. I recall that the Spanish architectural journal *El Croquis* also used this picture. When I told my mother that you could see the panties hanging on our veranda, she insisted they weren't hers, leading to a bit of an argument. When I returned to Rokko some time after moving away, I found that the hospital I had stayed at once as a child had been replaced by a building designed by Ando. Over the years the work of a single architect had gradually transformed my birthplace—you might say I grew up in tandem with that process. For better or worse, architecture has the power to radically alter the lives of the people it impinges on. I still recall that around the time I began working as an architect, many people were saying that architecture is a kind of violence. Rather than become oblivious to that aspect, I would like to think about how to accept it and still make something.

A mountain covered with stylish architect-designed buildings; the flimsy huts we built on the mountain, where the slightest breeze might blow them down; a bar where one could meet all kinds of people and share experiences with them—these are the things that still drive my design and construction work today.

Megu-chan was a girl one year younger than me who lived next door to the rental house I grew up in. Sometimes I went over to play at her house, and I remember wondering why someone else's house would smell so different from ours. I could see the second floor and the tile roof of Megu-chan's house from our second-floor window. When I opened the window during the pleasant spring and autumn seasons I would see Megu-chan on her roof reading a book. I still have a vivid memory of how she looked sprawled on the roof. Megu-chan was a mischievous girl and I heard that her grandmother would get so mad at her that she tied her to a chair. My friends and I would play baseball in the street in front of our house, shimmy up and down the downspout of a six-story apartment building, and crawl on all fours through a culvert. We'd hide our pocket money in the crevices of the stone wall of the drainage ditch. Objects and spaces may have an intended purpose, but as kids we saw them differently and put them to other uses as we pleased. In his book *Dying City, Recurring Town: New York and Beyond* (Ibunsha, 2010), the critic and translator Iwasaburo (Sabu) Kohso divides the elements that make up cities into two categories, *rokaku* (castle) and *chimata* (street). "Castle" refers to the infrastructure that sustains contemporary urban life—big buildings, expressways, railway networks, power plants—and is paid for by government and capital. "Street" refers to the parts of the city where people of all kinds gather and interact. The word *chimata* is said to derive from *michi no mata*, a fork in the road—in other words a junction or crossroads, a busy spot where people come and go, meet and depart. Sadly, there are few such spontaneous *chimata* among the streets and other public spaces of our cities today. But why can't we maintain the *chimata* approach of using our bodies to pursue alternative uses for the *rokaku*? In other words, change the "castle" into "streets." An easy-to-grasp example is skateboarding; others include parkour—the use of one's body to move rapidly among buildings and other structures—and train surfing, whose practitioners "surf" the roofs of moving trains. Artists Matthias Wermke and Mischa Leinkauf have expanded the relationship between the "castle" infrastructure and the body through such activities as riding the rails in their own self-built handcar or hanging a swing from a huge bridge.

In 2016 we carried out an experimental project, *researchlight*, that gave individuals the opportunity to intervene with their bodies in the "castle" and alter it. This was a work on the theme of infrastructure, which we submitted to the Spring 2016 edition of KYOTO EXPERIMENT (KEX), the Kyoto International Performing Arts Festival, in collaboration with the design studio UMA / design farm. An ubiquitous fact of life to us today, infrastructure has become a system that cannot be grasped in its entirety—just like the Google search engine. And just like a "castle," that infrastructure dictates much about our daily lives. ROHM Theatre Kyoto, one of the

KEX venues, is situated in Okazaki, a district on the eastern edge of the city that has been the site of numerous upheavals since the Heian era (794–1185). First urbanized during the Heian, it was reduced to ashes during the Onin War (1467–1477), flourished during the Edo period (1603–1867) as home to many feudal lords, then burned down again in the civil war that ended the Shogunate. Later, when the Lake Biwa Canal was built through Okazaki, it became a hub of modern industry. This tumultuous history gave birth to many forms of infrastructure whose vestiges still remain. We selected several examples, surveyed and measured them, and built life-size replicas in the public space known as ROHM Square. Among the infrastructural elements we selected were a dam from the canal, a bridge, a switch box, a stone wall remnant of Hosshoji temple, parts of the roof and torii gate of Heian Shrine, the handrail of a footpath, a baseball field scoreboard, the foundation stone of a long gone octagonal nine-story pagoda, and a U-shaped drainage ditch. These objects all served a function in the urban infrastructure, but the purpose of the project was to sever them from that context and function, and study how people would put them to use when presented in their pure form. These cut-up life-size elements ultimately became a playground for children. The Heian Shrine roof had just the right slope for a slide, so on holidays it was crawling with kids. Observing their behavior inspired us to modify some elements during the installation period in an attempt to encourage a diversity of activities like performances and skateboarding.

This book includes photos by Yusuke Nishimitsu, some from his portfolio and some that we asked him to take. For many years one of his subjects has been animals living in the city, or what he shyly calls the "urban wild"—wildlife surviving by utilizing the urban environment. Nishimitsu's birthplace, like mine, was near a mountain, albeit in a residential area, and he encountered many species of wildlife there. A family of mice lived in the attic of his house, though they did not pay for food or lodging. Another family, of wild boars, dug up the plant bulbs in the garden and ate them. All kinds of birds visited, as well as monkeys who played atop the wisteria trellis in the garden. Raccoons killed off all the carp in a neighbor's pond. The family of an elementary-school friend kept a pet crocodile that escaped and made the news when someone discovered it in a ditch. Apparently the crocodile

was placed in a zoo and the family that had owned it would go there and call it by name. Animals do not care about the purposes for which humans make things. Each one survives by observing and exploiting whatever conditions it encounters. As we go through our lives, the purposes of the things around us get imprinted on our minds. Instead of reacting unquestioningly to purposes devised by someone or other, why not think beyond them by approaching our environment with different techniques and modes of thought, as different animals do? Every time I pass by Heian Shrine, I picture kids sliding down the roof. It's an image I owe to Megu-chan, reading her book on the roof of the house next door.

"With Our Own Efforts"

In a house I used to live in, the stopper that covered the drain in the toilet tank broke apart. When you flushed the toilet, the water didn't stop, so every time you flushed you had to stick your hand in the tank to cover up the drain. It was a very old toilet, so they probably didn't sell that particular part any more. About four months before the toilet broke, the water flow to the washing machine became very sluggish, so I would carry water in a pot and dump it into the washer. The upshot was frequent trips back and forth between the kitchen and the veranda where the washer sat. Eventually the washer would no longer fill with water, so I washed my clothes by hand in the bathtub, using the washer only for the spin cycle. Finally the spin mechanism broke too, so I had to wring the clothes out by hand in the bathtub after washing them.

The cultural anthropologist Takeshi Matsushima, who teaches in the Graduate School of Social Sciences at Hiroshima University, once told me about Alfred Sohn-Rethel's "philosophy of the broken," which the Italian philosopher Giorgio Agamben discusses in his book *Nudities*. Most Japanese, I would say, get annoyed when their train or bus is late, or when something they use every day breaks down. People in Naples, Italy, on the other hand (though I doubt this is true for all of them), get irritated when systems work smoothly without any interruption, we are told. Where does this irritation come from? My hunch is that if you are deprived of the opportunity to commit your body or mind to a given system, you don't feel like you're really connected to it. In other words, when something is broken, it allows you to intervene with your own body or mind. A smooth-running system is annoying because it doesn't provide that opportunity. Intervention gives birth to the act of making something yourself. There is a similar phenomenon in Cuba. In 1961, after the Cuban Revolution toppled a pro-American regime, U.S. President Dwight D. Eisenhower cut diplomatic ties with the country, and all the American engineers there left. Then, when Cuba's ally the Soviet Union collapsed, it was faced with a severe shortage of goods. Cubans responded to these crises by learning how to do things for themselves: mending tears, repairing broken items, converting parts for use in other kinds of machinery. It's said that people would grill meat on the seat of a metal chair, seal up the bottom of a car to make a boat, add a simple engine and a plastic bottle for a gas tank to turn a bicycle into a motorbike. In 1992 the Cuban Army published a book titled *With Our Own Efforts*, a compendium of the repairing, remodeling, and recycling wisdom of ordinary citizens, thus making it available to everyone. Among other things the book contains a recipe for making a steak out of grapefruit rind. In this way a lack of goods and experts spawned a nation of amateur engineers and inventors. Today we have fewer opportunities than ever to make something on our own. Most of us live in rental housing that we are

contract-bound to restore to its original state when we move out. Thus compelled to avoid making any changes in the status quo, we feel like interlopers in our own homes. The relationship between our body and the place we are in becomes awkward. As for electrical appliances and cars, the computers embedded in them make it next to impossible to repair them ourselves. But even if that weren't so, we would still be unlikely to try our hand at repairs. Instead, when something malfunctions we discard it and buy a new one. Industrialization and mass production have left us with nothing else to do except focus on human relations and communication. In our utter lack of interest in committing to the mechanisms of things, the biggest loser, perhaps, is the body. The Italians and Cubans, as well as the Japanese in the immediate postwar years, had something invaluable: a do-it-yourself attitude.

As part of the Water and Land Niigata Art Festival held in Niigata City in 2015, we built a bridge to a small island in Fukushima Lagoon. On a visit to the site beforehand, we dropped in on a meeting of a citizens' group held in a vinyl greenhouse next to the lagoon. With architects and artists suddenly converging on the area to build various structures and works for the festival, local residents probably were feeling more anxiety than enthusiasm. In the greenhouse we were fed delicacies like bear collagen and small fish from the lagoon while we listened to people tell us things like, "The lagoon is beautiful just as it is. Don't build anything stupid." Indeed, Fukushima Lagoon is a wintering spot for migrating birds and a truly lovely place. Some sort of architectural structure might well be an eyesore. But then one of the members of the citizens' group, a gentleman who went by the name of Gotto-san, said, "How about building a boat?"—and that is what we decided to do then and there.

According to *Toyosaka City Folklore Survey Report I: River Boats of Toyosaka— Boatbuilding Methods* (1987), "Fukushima Lagoon was once surrounded by wetlands with countless waterways large and small flowing through the rice paddies and villages. These waterways served the function of roads, so river boats were an essential means of transportation. [. . .] The conversion of arable land to drained paddies and the development of ground transportation transformed life around the lagoon, and the river boats have all but disappeared. Today they are only used on occasion for fishing in the lagoon." From this we learned that river boats were once built in great numbers. When we asked how these boats were made, we were told that only one boatbuilder who knew the traditional methods remained in the town. We tried to set up a meeting with him right away, but he said he was too busy to help, so we promptly gave up on the idea of building a traditional boat. It was easy to do that because it turned out that Gotto-san and his friends also built river boats, just not in the traditional way. They made their boats with ample amounts of butyl tape, caulking, and rubber sheeting sold at the local home improvement center, and we thought that sounded even more fun. Gotto-san, who had been a carpenter, used to make his boats with leftover construction materials. We don't need first-

class technical skills (though we acknowledge their value). It's more our style to figure out how to solve problems by making use of the materials on hand, without worrying about tradition. So we quickly signed on as apprentices to Gotto-san et al. In June 2015 dot architects member Wataru Doi showed up at Fukushima Lagoon and spent ten intensive days learning how to build a contemporary version of a river boat. At the Osaka office of dot architects we built three eight-meter-long boats, shipped them to Niigata, and floated them on the lagoon. There we lashed them together to form a bridge to a small

island, thus creating a new walking course at the lagoon. When we left the site, Gotto-san gave Doi his favorite plane, which Doi still treasures and uses at various worksites. We usually make it a point to avoid meddling in spheres of activity other than those we customarily engage in. This time we had no idea we would wind up building boats, but once we tried, we found we could. The use of home improvement center materials and do-it-yourself troubleshooting are methods better suited to this "give it a try" mentality than are the skills of a specialist. As for the boats we built, we gave one to the citizens' group and another sits quietly on the approach to the Fukushima Lagoon Museum designed by Jun Aoki. We don't know what happened to the third one.

Gaps in the Window

I lived in a rented house at the foot of Mt. Rokko in Kobe with my parents, my younger brother, and my paternal grandmother. I think the house was built when the Hankyu Railway was extended into the area in the late 1920s, and I have heard that at first it stood alone in the middle of a field. It was a two-story wooden structure in the pseudo-Western style favored by carpenters in those days. When I lived there it was already old and the wooden fixtures no longer fit well, so there were gaps between all the windows and their frames. During the winter the curtains blew in the draft through the gaps, and I always thought it felt warmer outdoors than indoors. On windy days the entire house groaned as if some unknown entity were sharing the house with us or constantly entering and leaving it. I remember finding that scary when I was a kid. Ants would parade in lines across the veranda, slugs would crawl through the rooms, mice would scamper around the attic, and there were always centipedes, spiders and geckos in the house. Ivy also found its way in. While I was in college my grandmother died, and a few days after the funeral

we cleaned the small tatami-mat room and closet she had used. As elsewhere in the house there was a big gap between the window and its frame, and it looked like rain had been pouring in. Some paper had been wadded up and stuffed in the gap as packing. When my mother removed the clump of paper and spread it out, she looked aghast. The sheet was a page from my father's graduation album. There is something bracing about this attitude of using whatever's available—even a scrap of a precious family memory—either for some compelling reason, or because you view objects around you only in terms of their location and usefulness. What's there is for the use of whoever lives there. The layout of the resources we depend on for our lives is predetermined. To access oil, iron ore, and other resources extracted in some far-off place, we must have them transported via complex systems that the average citizen has no say in. Every day we use the materials provided by those systems for our livelihood, not the materials in our immediate vicinity. I'm not suggesting that pages from a graduation album should be a recyclable resource; I'm asking whether we are still capable of using the things around us as materials or foodstuffs.

According to the Ministry of Transport's *Road Statistics Yearbook 2019*, Japan's roads occupy 7,710 square kilometers of area—nearly the size of Shizuoka Prefecture. I can't help fantasizing about tearing up all that asphalt (well, not all of it) and growing food and materials there instead. Italy is said to have a large number of autonomous alternative spaces, known as "social centers," which people establish by illegally occupying empty houses, shuttered businesses and so on. Locals gather there and run their own libraries, language schools, live music venues, self-defense classes, restaurants, cafes and whatnot. (My source is Shinya Kitagawa, "Creating an Autonomous Space of Social Center in Milan, Italy: Between Social Inclusion and Autonomy," in *Studies in Urban Cultures* Vol. 14, 2012.) Of course they sometimes must deal with adverse circumstances like eviction. I think their point of departure is to ask the simple question, "Why shouldn't social centers be able to occupy places in the neighborhood that nobody else is using?"

During the Summer segment of the 2016 Setouchi Triennale, dot architects participated in a Creator in Residence program in the Sakate district of Shodoshima. The site for installing our work had already been prepared: a vacant lot with a shed on it partway up the hill. We decided to build a boardwalk there connecting the mountain to the sea. We were inspired by a text we learned about from Professor Shuichi Kawashima of the International Research Institute of Disaster Science at Tohoku University: "There is a custom of gazing at the sea, as if waiting for a letter, whenever one has time to spare" (Toshio Tanabe, *The Seashore: Kochi*

Historical Photography 1, Kochi Municipal Library, 1993). These words have the ring of truth about life by the sea. In the past, Japan's coastal communities existed as part of an unbroken continuum from sea to houses to mountain. Then the postwar recovery and boom decades ushered in the construction of coastal roads to improve distribution and seawalls to ensure safety. These projects helped grow the economy and prevent natural disasters, but they also severed the link between sea and land. The urge to reestablish that link by hurdling over the infrastructure inserted by past planners inspired us with the idea of building a boardwalk from high on the hill down to the shore. There are many evocative passages written about the sea; this one by Kunio Yanagita, from *Paths over the Sea* (Kadokawa Bunko, 2013), talks about driftwood:

> We can no longer imagine a time when the mountains and valleys of our country were covered with huge trees that would be carried down to the sea by the forces of nature. The water once supplied us with a far greater abundance of things than it brings today. Every small offshore island had its sacred mountain, cherished since ancient times, and rather than put an axe to those forests, people long relied on driftwood of all sizes to build their houses and stoke their fires.

Yanagita describes a lifestyle in which people picked up all kinds of objects washed ashore by the sea and used them as materials for survival. In Ryuta Imafuku's essay "Fragment of a (Parallel) Constitution for a Harmonious Archipelago Society" (in *The Latent Power of a Constitution in the Republican Society of the Ryukyu Islands: Ideas about Archipelago, Asia, and Borders*, Miraisha, 2014), he introduces a concept he calls "giving up." The occupation of territory gave birth to the concept of ownership. I think Imafuku uses the term "giving up" to describe, not the elimination of ownership by communal sharing, nor abandonment per se, but rather a state of release accompanied by thoughtful coexistence, a sort of tenancy if you will. Both these concepts of "picking up" and "giving up" remind us that the land and sea preceded humans, who exist amid a vast natural environment of things both organic and inorganic, and who would be wiser not to alter that environment by their own hand. "As if waiting for a letter," people once upon a time waited for the sea to bring them something or someone, and as if sending a letter, they would see people and things off to sea as well. For this project we cut down trees on the mountain in back, stripped off the bark, and used the green wood for our posts and beams. The planks came from a wrecked boat. It was only a small boardwalk, but as we built it we could gaze at the sea before us, or turn around and see the mountain behind us. The link we felt with nature made us think about the meaning of taking time to make something with materials found where you are.

Japan's forestry industry is facing hard times these days. To deal with the housing shortage after the war, the government implemented a policy of cutting

down the country's broadleaf forests and replacing them with plantations of cedar and cypress to serve as building materials. Then, during the rapid industrialization and mass production of the subsequent boom years, people left the mountains for the cities to find work, and forestry workers' wages rose in tandem with the wages for urban labor. When Japan switched from a fixed to a floating currency exchange rate, cheap lumber from abroad began flooding the country and demand for domestic timber fell. If you try to buy logs directly from a lumber market now, you will probably be turned down. It's a strange state of affairs when there are literally mountains of building materials growing everywhere, yet they can't be put to use. No longer can the inhabitants of a place use the things growing there for themselves. Every time I ponder the complex causes of this situation, I remember my father's graduation album.

Tools in Hand

If you want to make something, you need tools. In his book *Tools for Conviviality*, the philosopher Ivan Illich defines two categories of tools for making things. One is the industrial tool—the kind adapted to the logic of mass production. Such tools are highly specialized, so not just anyone can use them. The other is the hand tool—the hammer, saw, or power tool that anyone can use with ease to achieve their personal objectives. These tools expand the scope of our freedom and enhance the diversity of our lives. The haves and the have-nots use different tools. At dot architects we have no land, no factory, no machines, so we make everything with hand tools. Naturally our products lack the perfection of manufactured goods, but that's not a problem. Industrial products have the characteristic of differentiating makers from users. Products predicated on mass production cannot accommodate the peculiar needs of individual users; they must be designed for ease of use by the great majority. Hand-tooled products, on the other hand, can be repaired or altered on the spot. That attribute allows users to participate by modifying tools for themselves, thus eliminating the user-maker distinction. This way of thinking can be applied to many fields of endeavor, not just products.

In 2013, as part of the Setouchi Triennale arts festival, we built a small community gathering place, which we dubbed UmakiCamp, in the Umaki district on the island of Shodoshima, Kagawa Prefecture. Initially we were told that it would be dismantled when the festival ended. Our model for the project was the Citizens Media Center built on the occasion of the G8 Summit in 2008 at Lake Toya, Hokkaido as an outlet for information from non-mass media perspectives. It was a place where citizens could spontaneously disseminate and share information ignored by the mass media. At UmakiCamp we built the physical equivalent: an alternative

public space that we hoped would afford local people the opportunity to spontaneously gather and carry out civic activities that could not get backing from existing
institutions. Shodoshima is the largest island in the Seto Inland Sea not connected
to the mainland by a bridge. The biggest problem it currently faces is depopula-
tion, with a declining birthrate and a growing proportion of elderly citizens. If the
islanders wish to preserve the rich natural environment, scenery, industries, social
services and schools with which they are blessed, they must create their own conditions autonomously, without relying on anyone else. Needless to say we designed
the camp's meeting hall, with the help of structural engineer Eisuke Mitsuda, so
that we could build it ourselves. By using a contemporary version of post-in-ground
construction, sinking the pillars into holes dug in the concrete foundation, you can
finish the framework in a day with stepladders—no scaffolding or temporary en-
closures. But simply building an empty box and calling it a building doesn't make it
useful unless someone knows how to use it. Therefore, while we were building the
hall, we also prepared various media that would connect local people with tourists
and with each other. One such medium was film. The Neighborhood Film Club, a
filmmaking workshop conducted by the NPO remo (Record, Expression and Medium
Organization), works by dividing participants from a neighborhood association or the
like into groups whose members jointly plan a script, casting, cameras, props and
costumes, then make a film in only one day. When we proposed this sort of workshop to people in Umaki, however, they all looked at us with dubious expressions.
"We believe in doing things right, so we'd want to prepare in advance." "Instead of
dividing into groups, why can't we all work on one film together?" We immediately
agreed to their suggestions and modified the workshop method accordingly. Then,
a script was found in the drawer of a cabinet in the local community center. It was
for a play titled *Sympathies*, a parody of the film *Departures*. The community had a
custom of presenting plays at events for senior citizens. A bit of research reveals
that this was a longstanding tradition, part of what is described by a document
from the wartime government's Culture Division as "the theater movement in
Yasuda Village, Shodoshima" under the category
"Amateur Theater" in *Collected Materials: Total
War and Culture, Volume 1: The Culture Division of
the Imperial Rule Assistance Association and the
Cultural Support Campaign* (Kenzo Kitagawa, ed.,
Otsuki Shoten, 2000):

> Our thinking is that Japan's traditions are best
> preserved in its farming villages; that these vil-
> lages, as the linchpin of the nation's strength,
> must be improved if the nation is to grow
> stronger; and that the key to such improvement

is culture. Sadly, however, culture is the very thing most overlooked in the villages. We have been discussing these issues for some time while simultaneously making them the basis for a campaign.

Though Yasuda is in a different part of the island, one can imagine the same activities taking place in Umaki. I was impressed to learn that, during a period when freedom of speech and cultural activity was all but extinct, there were circumstances under which one could still assert that culture was the most important thing. "Farmers' Kabuki" stages can be found on Shodoshima in the villages of Hitoyama and Nakayama, and even today they are used once a year for large festive Kabuki productions by local residents. I went to see the Farmers' Kabuki in Hitoyama many times. You descend some steps from the road to a space next to a shrine, where you find the stage facing a broad seating area terraced in lawn-covered tiers, each about 1.5 meters wide. There is also raised seating along the sides of the lawn. The buildings and even the railings are low-slung in pleasing proportions, with the shrine, stage, and raised seating all enclosing the lawn like a natural extension of the terrain, forming a unified space. Everybody brings their own box lunch and the atmosphere is truly festive. We emulated this layout at UmakiCamp. Instead of exposing the entire yard to the road, we placed a goat hut by the roadside to partially block the view and, to give the space a unified feel, enclosed it with the main volume of the meeting hall, a farmhouse, and the stone wall of a temple. Farmers' Kabuki is organized by annual rotation among the residents of each locale, who prepare for their performance with intense rehearsing. Contemporary quips like "I drank too much at the bar last night" are inserted into the dialogue of classic plays to howls of laughter. My guess is that daily life could sometimes feel stifling in small villages where everyone was related by land or blood, and that performances like Kabuki in which you could play the part of someone else provided a kind of stress release. I once heard on the radio that back when Farmers' Kabuki was a widespread phenomenon, government officials tried to ban it as a frivolous waste of the peasants' time, to which the peasants responded that their performances were an offering to the gods. They got to keep their Kabuki. In any era, life means little if you can't have some fun.

Returning to the subject of filmmaking, the script titled *Sympathies* had been stashed away because it was about funerals, a topic some thought inappropriate for an elderly audience. A few weeks after the decision to turn it into a film, the scenario was reborn as "*Sympathies*, a nostalgic comedy arbitrarily submitted to the Setouchi Triennale." Nowadays most funerals are held in a hall, but at one time, neighbors would join together to convert the house of the deceased into a funeral parlor, thus giving them a sendoff from their own home. This film was about one such funeral. One notable scene involved removing the fusuma sliding panels that demarcated the rooms in the house; one of the virtues of a traditional Japanese

residence is its versatility, since you can expand or shrink the space in this way. The film was basically a serious story interspersed with corny gags worthy of a Yoshimoto New Comedy production. The famous filmmaker and comedian Beat Takeshi even watched it and gave it a thumbs-up. Local people took nearly all of the 30 roles in the cast. Shooting began at 9 a.m. and wrapped up at 2 p.m. After editing, we screened the film in the UmakiCamp yard that same evening. Local folks showed up in force, and the village of Umaki echoed with laughter. I was offered the part of Mortician B. Whether it's architecture or entertainment, it's better not to wait for someone to do it for you. We wanted to test whether it was possible to create something with simple tools if we all worked together, even if it was just on a small scale. Since we didn't set up a temporary fence during construction, kids on their way home from school would come over to make things with wood remnants, and neighbors would drop by with snacks or with plantings for the yard. Local residents kept watch over the building process from start to finish. Moreover, UmakiCamp was not built on public land, but on private property owned by Mr. Yukio Shiota, former mayor of Shodoshima Town. The result was a common space, open to all, created through cooperation by the public and private sectors—assistance from the town combined with what was no doubt a longstanding tradition of community solidarity. At the time, Mr. Shiota wrote in his blog:

> With UmakiCamp, which represented the novel concept of a general-use community center not under government jurisdiction, I thought we could engage in a social experiment that might solve a number of problems, notably in the social safety-net areas of welfare, education, and health.

It was decided that UmakiCamp would continue as a small social experiment even after the Setouchi Triennale was over. It still stands in Umaki, thought it has not seen much active use lately. Now, however, we are working in Umaki on a different project whose instigator has expressed an interest in putting UmakiCamp to use. In all its phases, from construction to filmmaking, UmakiCamp has been indebted to local residents, and to the members of the community organization Umaki Hishio-kai.

Okonomiyaki

My friend the poet Yoshinori Henguchi tells of how, when the family no longer had income from his father, his mother suddenly decided to open an okonomiyaki shop. Business was good and the shop was drawing regular customers, but then his mother fell ill, and Henguchi had to take over. At first he was so bad at it that he

drove customers away, but after half a year he became adept at cooking the savory pancakes and business improved again.

Takaaki Kihara, who works at the same university as I do, was raised in a single-mother household. His mother worked part-time while raising him and his sister. When Kihara was in the third grade his mother suddenly asked, "Is it all right if I come home late?" Kihara got nervous thinking she was going to take on some sort of risky night job, but it turned out that she'd spent all her savings to open an okonomiyaki shop. Now, twenty-some years later, the shop is still going strong, and the four ladies about the same age as Kihara's mother who started out as part-timers when it opened are still working there. I never liked okonomiyaki much myself. For one thing, having been raised in the Kansai region, I frequently had to eat it for lunch, so it lost its appeal. But after hearing stories like these I realized I should pay okonomiyaki some respect. Not only is it tasty, but it makes for an excellent vocation. Okonomiyaki is the ultimate griddle food. It's predictable in a good way, just like the endless repetition of the same gags by the Yoshimoto New Comedy troupe. Their jokes are funny because the actors on stage are so good at what they do. Their delivery is spot-on, utterly unlike lines tossed off by some novice getting by on his good looks.

Let's subject okonomiyaki to some analysis. The base ingredients are wheat flour, soup stock, egg, cabbage, maybe some fried batter. Then you add your favorite ingredients to taste. Each shop offers its own set of options to choose from, but there is no novelty in them whatsoever; every item is something you can find anywhere. The only tools you need are a cutting board, kitchen knife, bowl, spatula, and griddle. None require any particular skill. And the only techniques are cutting, mixing, grilling, and flipping. Nothing could be simpler.

With such basic, accessible ingredients, tools and skills, it's easy to "just give it a try." A single order of okonomiyaki is relatively cheap, so most people find it affordable. These factors allow for an okonomiyaki experience that varies from shop to shop. Some places leave it to the customers to grill their order themselves from start to finish, so it's hard to say who actually made the dish. Customers eat straight from the grill, so they get their food while it's hot, along with a direct hit of the smell and sound of sizzling sauce. One day at an okonomiyaki shop I frequent, I heard a rustling sound coming from the elderly couple at the next table. Peering over, I saw one of them take some curry powder out of a bag and pour a generous portion into the batter. The aroma of curried okonomiyaki—definitely not a menu item—soon filled the shop. Some serious customizing there. Okonomiyaki also has regional variants, and within the Kansai region one can find shops offering different ingredient blends and grilling methods.

Easy-to-get ingredients, tools anyone can handle, simple techniques, ease of execution, diversity by shop and region, customization that doesn't mess

with the basic template . . . doesn't okonomiyaki sound like a metaphor for architecture? As a matter of fact, okonomiyaki is one of the architectural inspirations for dot architects. We think of architecture as a point of convergence by numerous factors, and okonomiyaki is nothing if not a vivid example of such convergence.

Panini

This is a story I heard from a colleague at the university where I teach, the ceramist Toshio Matsui. While studying at a university in Italy in the 1980s, he would often skip class and head for a billiard parlor, across from which there was a street vendor selling panini. A single panini sold for 500 lira. One day he ordered a panini and handed over a 1,000 lira note, but the vendor was out of change. Without hesitating, the vendor tore the note in half and returned one half as change. Some time later Matsui went to purchase a panini again and handed over the remaining half of the note. The vendor took it, taped it to the other half, which he still had, and stuck it in his pocket.

We tend to assume that money must not be torn up, but if we think of the value of paper money as based on its surface area, rather than belonging to the object as a whole, we should be able to subdivide it as we please. I thought a lot about why the panini vendor was able to do such a clever thing. This is just a guess, but perhaps it's because he was accustomed to tearing the panini by hand. Money is an abstract entity, so a physical object representing it cannot be broken up. If we do wish to break it, we have to exchange it for money of a different value. It's a rather tedious process if you think about it. Panini, on the other hand, is strictly an object, so if you want to tear off a bit to feed the pigeons, you can. A single panini thus highlighted the tedium of the global currency system. By temporarily converting objects and actions into currency and calculating their value according to the quantity of that currency, we can exchange them for just about anything else and transcend the limits of physical distance. Currency is an impressive invention, but it inserts an extra step that dilutes the connection between an object or action and the next object or action one acquires. When the place we acquire currency and the place we spend it are not the same, it deprives of us of the capacity to envision what lies beyond objects and actions. The way the panini vendor handled money gives us some other food for thought as well. Money by itself serves no use; only when it is exchanged for something else does it acquire meaning. In other words, when we talk about "using" money, we don't really mean using money the physical object. The most famous example of literally using money may be the old caricature of an elderly nouveau-riche customer setting fire to a banknote so he can look for his shoes in a fancy, dimly-lit restaurant. The panini vendor decided of his own

accord that even when using money as a medium of exchange, you can treat it as an object of certain dimensions and tear it in half to halve its value. It gets complicated when you mix an abstraction like the currency system with a concrete act like ripping an object into pieces, but the notion of inserting that concrete act into the process is intriguing. I realize that abstraction is a great human invention, but it also separates things from their use. This is true of the land we live on as well. Until the early-modern era, land was inseparably linked to its "use," such as for production or habitation. In the words of Kunio Niwa, which appear in *Land and Humans: A Historical Approach to Contemporary Land Issues* (Hiroyuki Kotani, Matori Yamamoto, and Susumu Fujita; Yushisha, 2012):

> Land ownership by peasants in the early-modern era was a clearcut relationship, consisting of the actual occupation and use of the land. In other words, a direct physical connection to the land—living in the house one built there, tilling one's own fields, utilizing the water and woodland resources there— [. . .] defined peasant land ownership during that period, and consequently someone of non-peasant social status could not become a landowner.

The authors add that this concept is evident in the traditional land-allotment system under which cropland was redistributed among the peasantry by lottery every few years. Under this system, land was not "owned" by the individual, but "used" jointly by a community. However, when land-tax reform based on the one-parcel, one-owner principle was implemented in the modern era, it gave legal legitimacy to the notion that land was private property and could be bought or sold at will. You could now own land whether you used it or not, thus severing the relationship between land and its use. Today Japan is full of abandoned land of unknown ownership, as well as land and houses that are owned by someone but utterly vacant. Why isn't such land utilized for our livelihoods? Unused spaces should be liberated and converted to places for use by small communities in each town. During the 1970s the New York artist Liz Christy occupied a rubble-strewn vacant lot and began "guerilla gardening" there, turning it into a gathering place for people in the neighborhood. This action demonstrated how gardening could serve to foster a local community, but its real significance is as an example of putting "unused" land to use. The same can be said of Italy's social centers, where people have illegally occupied unused public buildings or factories and transformed them into places for use by everyone.

Most of us spend the money we receive for our labor on a place—either as

rent or as repayment of a home loan. That state of affairs reinforces our conscious-
ness of individual ownership and banishes thoughts of co-ownership, rendering
impermissible the use of land for free, even vacant land. We should instead think
of land and its use as a unit, and further consider the sharing of rights to that unit
among many people. Institutionalization of such an approach, however, would bring
with it other problems. Ideally we should create situations, even temporarily, under
conditions we have devised by our own efforts—modest intrusions, on a par with
that of the panini vendor. Today, as with land, our access to many of the things that
surround us is restricted to their final "use" or to the "receiving" of services. I would
like to contemplate what sort of architecture we might create to serve as a point of
convergence where people, things, and the environment are in actual contact as we
directly access, assemble, and utilize resources.

The fields that once covered the riverbeds of Osaka are gone. But I believe that
even now, somewhere, people are opening up land to cultivate and use together.

On the Street

Azenbo Soeda was a *rokyoku*-style narrative singer and songwriter during the
Taisho era (1912–26). In a very short essay titled "Beggars Who Don't Beg" (in his
Record of the Asakusa Underworld, Kindai Seikatsu Sha, 1930), he depicts the lives
of street performers of various genres. Among them are a man with no fingers who
plucks the shamisen, and a philosopher-beggar who delivers amusing speeches
relating the theory of relativity to life on the street. The scenes and people he
describes are, without exception, cheerful and appealing. The animated film *Chie
the Brat* features many similar street scenes, but most of the characters are pretty
appalling. Even the heroine Chie's father Tetsu unhesitatingly beats on Chie's class-
mates. There are portrayals of people of a type one doesn't see much these days,
as well as of the various survival techniques they employ.

In high school I began working part-time for a construction company. There was
a guy there named Chiba. He was mainly a plumber, but also a gas fitter who did a
bit of carpentry, construction, and electrical work as well. He performed all these
jobs without a license—not even a driver's license, though he drove his light van
to work every day. He was a jack of all trades, but a master of none, an attribute
I liked. Nowadays we see licenses and qualifications proliferate in tandem with
the rampant specialization of the workplace. As the word "professional" signifies,
nothing less than top-notch work is acceptable, whatever the field. It is no longer
easy for one person to make a living as a jack of all trades. The upshot of this trend
is that after a career working for the same company, people retire to a life of lying
on the sofa bingeing on reruns of their favorite cop drama. Instead of staying home

all day watching TV, I think I'd rather be out on the street, running a small sidewalk business or something. That might also be one way to restore some of the neighborhood atmosphere that our all-too-clean cities have lost.

Until about three years ago I lived in a small maisonette on the third and fourth floor of a four-story apartment house. A fierce-looking fellow with dreadlocks lived on the second floor diagonally below my flat. One night I was walking home from the station, having taken the last train, when I saw the dreadlocked fellow puking into a planter in front of a bank. No doubt he had had a bit too much to drink. Another time a trail of bloodstains led up the stairs to this individual's door. Since his behavior didn't seem exactly exemplary, I tended to give him a wide berth. Then one day I was hanging one of my favorite shirts to dry on my balcony when a gust of wind blew it away. It landed on the balcony of the dreadlocked fellow. After hesitating for a minute I wrote a note asking him to hold on to the shirt, placed it in a bag with some sweets, and hung it on his doorknob. The next day there was a bag hanging on the doorknob with my shirt inside. What's more, the shirt had been carefully ironed and folded. I wrote a thank-you note and hung it with some beer and oranges on his doorknob. After that, whenever I put out my laundry or took it in, my eyes naturally wandered to the dreadlocked fellow's balcony. I noticed that it was often occupied by a tabby cat. Gradually my impression of this gentleman began to change. Then, one Sunday, three policemen came to my door and asked if I'd seen anyone suspicious. No, I replied. When I opened the door and cautiously checked out what was going on, however, it appeared that the dreadlocked guy had been harboring a criminal. From my window I actually saw the police pointing at and questioning the suspect. Not long afterward the dreadlocked fellow moved away, leaving the cat behind. For a while the cat lingered on around the apartment house, and the young man living in the opposite flat on the second floor would feed it canned fish. I sometimes gave it a little rice. Eventually, though, the cat disappeared too. I hope it's all right. We often hear that the apartment lifestyle today discourages any sense of community and that it's hard for people living alone to communicate

with one another, but occasionally interesting things do happen. Still, the only memories I retain from my time in that apartment house are of the dreadlocked fellow, and the heavy breathing of the fat chihuahua kept by the woman in the flat across from me. Only later did it occur to me that what the apartment house really needed was an alley.

The maisonette I was living in had begun to feel cramped. For that and other reasons I had spent about five years looking for land, or a condo, or a house to rent, but failed to find anything suitable. Apartments all had similar layouts and arrangements, and just

moving into a bigger one didn't seem like a life-altering move. I thought about buying land but started to think twice about that too. It occurred to me that I had never owned my own house or land. Perhaps it was because I'd lived in rented housing since I was born, but I began to feel uncomfortable about the notion of selling off the surface of the Earth in bits and pieces. Notwithstanding the fact that I prefer to live in the middle of a city right now, I think the right attitude to adopt is that you're going to borrow just a little bit of the Earth's surface. Perhaps I was trying to find a place for "lodging," with no clearcut "here" vs. "there," somewhere in a city.

While I was thinking these thoughts, I came upon an old wooden row house on an alley in downtown Osaka. It was 106 years old, one of five such row houses that did not burn down in the wartime fire-bombings of Osaka. There is no frontage road, and you have to make two turns down the alley to get there. If you look in the alley from the main road, it appears to dead-end at the rusty galvanized-iron wall of a row house. After the first turn, you see a wall covered by corrugated PVC sheeting with three or four holes in it. At your feet you can see bricks where thin bits of mortar have peeled off. Turning the second corner you come to the alley in front of our row house. The pavement is kept nice and clean, and has a small vegetable garden flanking it. Another house stands flush with the south side of the row house, but the north side opens onto a park. For such a small park it has a number of large trees—ginkgo, cherry, camphor—that give it a seasonal feel.

When I first set foot in the house I noticed the tatami-mat flooring had rotted and stank of the stray cats living there, but the structure seemed basically sound. The ground floor was damp and dark, but after talking it over with my partner, we decided to move into this old house anyway. The neighborhood grew up at the dead end of a canal dug during the Edo period (1603–1867) from the Okawa, a branch of the Yodo River, and was once occupied by a magnificent mountain of trash, I'm told. Early in the subsequent Meiji era it became the site of Osaka Prison. At that point the area was still outside Osaka City proper. Around the time of the Sino-Japanese War, Osaka began to flourish as a hub for commerce and industry, particularly spinning. The city grew in both area and population, absorbing the farming villages around it. The row house was built during this period of rapid urbanization, which transformed the meaning of "place" and the spatial arrangement of the city. Ever since then, relentless development has constantly reconfigured Osaka's city center. If you look up you see highrise condos encroaching on the sky; the row house survives like a tiny island in their midst. Vertically layered multi-unit housing serves its purpose as an invention that enables many people to live on a small plot of land, but there is much that we lose by being so detached from the ground. Let me quote a passage from *Fake Speech by the Head of the New Downtown Party*, a work in which contemporary artist Yasumasa Morimura impersonates a fictitious politician named Machishita Rojizo:

Anyway, there's a dog that pees on the phone pole right in front of my house.

[. . .] When I get up in the morning and go outside, there's always a dark spray of piss around the pole. Washing it away with a hose is one of my daily routines. If I don't watch my step, the entrance to my house starts to stink. Never failing to take care of your surroundings every day—that's the spirit of people living in old downtown neighborhoods.

In the course of watering the vegetables and cleaning the alley, one gets to consult on various matters with the other residents of the row house, which leads to helping each other out in little ways from day to day. The alley teaches us that a small world just 30 centimeters in front of our house connects us to an entire neighborhood. Nearby are old men and women who have lived there a long time, reminding us that we are also linked to people who live a bit apart from us.

Houses in general tend to face directly onto a street with traffic. If there is a yard between the house and the road, it's no more than a privately-owned buffer zone. The street itself is essentially an expanse of empty space set aside for the occasional passing car. A place where street and house directly abut each other cannot support a diversity of streetside activities. But little happenings are always occurring in a place like an alley, territory shared by the people living along it. Stray cats and old men I don't know stare at me through windows. Children peer into my house and yell out that it's a private eye's office. Dead leaves pile up in autumn, the guy next door can be heard practicing his golf putting, kids' backsides form a row as they squat behind the trees in front of our house while playing hide and seek. One of our neighbors has arbitrarily made a path, like an animal trail, as a shortcut to the park right across our vegetable patch. But after seeing him call "Here, kitty kitty" in a gentle voice and offer food to a stray cat, I can't stay mad at him. Night after night I watered a banana tree I planted in the park. When the leaves were torn off in a gale, it made me glad to hear a mother call out to her child the next day, "Look, the banana tree is broken."

Up to now, this alley and this row house have weathered the many changes buffeting the city. The environment may change even more over the next decade. What will happen to life on the alley, so close to the ground? How can we create more places like this alley, which once could be found everywhere? I want to ponder these questions here on the front lines as I share in the unforeseeable events perpetrated by living creatures like ourselves.

Under the Lawn

One night when I was a freshman in college, my dog began barking and wouldn't stop. In the early hours of the morning the Great Hanshin-Awaji Earthquake struck.

I leapt out of bed, but the shaking was so intense I couldn't do anything. Once it subsided, I looked around. The earthen wall of my room had collapsed, things were scattered everywhere, and the electricity and gas were cut off. Since the water still seemed to be running, I filled my bathtub. Then the water stopped too. As I was cleaning up the house the radio reported that someone had been injured by a falling television set. This was the first news I recall hearing about injuries from the quake. Soon, however, the extent of the damage began to grow with every report, until they were telling us that the Hanshin Expressway itself had toppled over. Several friends of mine lived nearby, so after cleaning up a bit I got on my scooter and headed out to see if they were all right. Just south of my house was a five-way intersection that marks the entrance to the Mt. Rokko hiking trail. The traffic signals were out, of course, but it was busy as usual. Standing in the center of the crossroads was a man directing traffic with his hands—not a policeman, just a middle-aged guy from the neighborhood. As I headed further south on my scooter, though, conditions changed rapidly. Houses were collapsed and burning, and someone was administering cardiac massage to someone else by the roadside. I drove through this hellish scene, checking to make sure that my friends had safely made it to an evacuation center. One classmate from middle school pulled people from the rubble, then headed for a collapsed department store to retrieve goods from inside. Streets and sidewalks had disappeared. There was no water, no electricity, no gas: the infrastructure had shut down. Local residents stood in line to get water from a well at the temple up the hill. A friend whose house had a propane-gas bath let everyone bathe there. Someone who could still boil rice made rice balls and delivered them to an evacuation center. People struggled to survive by cooperating on a level transcending everyday rules and standards of right and wrong. Though problems inevitably cropped up, it seemed to be a lesson in how communities are born. It made me, a student in a university law department, realize that rules are not something to obey, but something we make up ourselves.

The neighborhood I grew up in was also home to the headquarters of the Yamaguchi-gumi, Japan's largest yakuza organization. The group held memorial services for its members at the Shinto shrine by the road I took to elementary school, and I remember having to take a different route on those days. But overall, the presence of the Yamaguchi-gumi and its mansion, built in the delta formed by two rivers, was just a part of our daily lives. Their neighbors suffered no harm, and sometimes they bought juice for kids like me. It was a safe neighborhood, and one could not help thinking of the gang as one more crime-deterring force besides the police. In the aftermath of the

quake, when starving residents were waiting for National Self-Defense Force troops to arrive with food, the Yamaguchi-gumi was there doling out bread before the SDF showed up. A long line formed in front of their headquarters, and everybody got some bread. I stood in that line too, bag in hand. A tough-looking fellow was handing the bread out, but when I presented my bag with one hand, he said, "Use both hands. Your manners are bad, so you only get one piece." I admired them for maintaining their sense of etiquette in such dire circumstances. A sign with big letters saying "Throw out the gangs" stood over a stream near their mansion. But it was just a sign; I doubt that anyone in the neighborhood seriously felt that way. I actually think it was good that an organization existed in my neighborhood that operated on principles utterly different from those we learned in school.

In *Poétique de la Relation*, the Caribbean-born author Édouard Glissant writes of how the Caribbean, which unlike the more homogeneous Mediterranean has an archipelago of numerous islands, forms a network of diverse places and conditions that coexist with one another. In my town's coexistence with the Yamaguchi-gumi, and in the Caribbean archipelago, one can see a state of equilibrium gradually achieved through repeated adjustments of a relationship that waxes and wanes. Problems that crop up from day to day, and the time it takes to resolve them, may be an annoyance, yet that process also gives people something to grab onto when both sides reach out to each other. Lately, however, we live our lives atop a smooth expanse of lawn that covers up any such irregularities, and we seem to have lost that state of equilibrium.

In the postscript to his book *A Positive Theory of the Modern Yakuza: 90 Years of the Yamaguchi-gumi* (Chikuma Shobo, 2007), Manabu Yamazaki writes that the modern yakuza gang was like a nonprofit organization that looked after people who had fallen through the cracks in the system. The Great Hanshin-Awaji Earthquake occurred in January. As I rode my scooter along a sidewalk that was still in a state of disrepair in March, I heard the speaker from a patrol car blare, "You can't do that any more!" The notion of a "disaster utopia" notwithstanding, the various roles and rules that emerged in the aftermath of the earthquake have gradually faded away, and in some locales, the frantic pace of reconstruction has severed any bonds of neighborliness and solidarity that once existed there.

Fragment in a Vacant Lot

Next door to the rental house I grew up in was our landlord's house, which had a large garden with so many trees that it resembled a little forest. The garden even contained a small shrine at which the landlord prayed every morning. My mother said that the old man had told her many times about seeing *kappa*—the

mythical water sprites—play catch with balls of fire under the veranda. Back then people still had the capacity to imagine the presence of such creatures in familiar circumstances. Nowadays, when everything is brightly lit and Japanese houses don't even have verandas, where is a *kappa* to play? The *Tsukumogami-emaki*, a picture scroll said to date back to the Muromachi period (1336–1573), depicts how old tools discarded at year's end would become inhabited by spirits who took pleasure in attacking the tools' owners. I think it's extremely important to preserve a sensibility capable of imagining not only humans but tools engaging in bizarre behavior.

As the modernization process transformed Japan's politics, economics, and social geography, the capitalist system that came to predominate from the late 19th century on supplied inexpensive goods in vast quantities through improved production efficiency and standardization. This led to the invention of a radical methodology: the conversion of workers themselves into magnets for consumption. The growing standardization of products gave birth to "design," which emphasized exclusiveness. It's hard to imagine *tsukumogami* inhabiting such products.

After the old landlord died his family sold the property, and both the house and garden were torn down. Before any new construction began my mother snuck into the lot, which was now completely vacant, and came back with a shard of porcelain about five centimeters square that had been hidden in the grass. It was a piece of a basin in which everyone had washed their faces each morning when the entire family still lived there. Today the family is scattered and some of them are no longer alive. Why are we moved by the presence of a tiny fragment of an everyday object?

Once I was given a guided tour of the basement of The Museum of Kyoto by curator Masakage Murano. It was lined with cases of relics unearthed quite by chance after sleeping undisturbed for hundreds or thousands of years. However one may evaluate them, these objects are nothing more than fragments, but they

survive as vestiges of the activities of people who may be nameless but who once indubitably existed. There are many more such fragments still asleep even deeper in the ground. Though the *tsukumogami* may have vanished, our history lives on in little objects scattered all over the place. Instead of wasting our time lamenting a world that's drowning in throwaway goods, let's free our imagination to inhabit those tiny, inconsequential fragments.

Cherry Tree Tales

A single cherry tree grew out of the road right in front of the house where I was born and raised. The blossoms that covered it every spring were beautiful, so we posed under them for photos whenever the family went out together, or to mark the start of the new school year. For me and everyone in the neighborhood the cherry blossoms were a familiar sight that repeated without fail year after year. Eventually, though, the owner of our rented house died and his family sold the land for cash. Both the landlord's house and the one I lived in were demolished. Today a drab prefab low-rise condo built by a commercial builder stands there. When they were putting up the condo, we heard that they were planning to cut down the cherry tree because it was in the way. It did, after all, grow right out of the road. However, people in the neighborhood who looked forward to the tree's annual blooming were not happy about this. At a local women's club meeting, one woman declared it to be a historic cherry tree that had been admired by the emperor when he visited the area. Everybody got on board that bandwagon, and the tree still stands there today. Of course the tale was a complete fabrication. The real story as I heard it took place before I was born. Our landlord apparently had a nurseryman bring him two cherry trees. He planted one in his garden, but when the nurseryman asked him what to do with the remaining tree, the landlord replied, "Just plant it in the road or

something." And so he did.

The set of handscrolls known as the *Illustrated Legends of Ishiyama-dera Temple* contains a tale in which the priest Roben, while clearing land for the temple, found a large bell buried in the ground and, deeming this auspicious, built a shrine for the bell. In this way he took something that he happened to dig up and used it as justification for expanding his project. Tales are a powerful thing. True or not, they often serve as the engine driving major events.

During the 2013 Setouchi Triennale, *ANGER from the Bottom*, a huge moving sculpture 6.5 meters tall of a monster rising out of a well, was installed in the Sakate district on Shodoshima island. Created by filmmaker Beat Takeshi and artist Kenji Yanobe, the work occupies the remains of an old well and is intended to sound a warning about the current state of relations between humanity and nature. When Beat Takeshi visited the island, the townspeople conducted a "water god dedication ceremony," a Shinto ritual to enshrine the sculpture as the god of rain and flood control. After the Triennale was over, there was a strong sentiment among the townspeople to preserve the work and its natural setting in perpetuity.

Community and business leaders in Shodoshima Town and residents of the Sakate district formed the Beat Shrine Construction Association to build a sanctuary that would protect the sculpture from the elements without disrupting the natural environment. (The shrine's Japanese name, Biito, is a pun: it's pronounced like Takeshi's name, but the characters mean "beautiful shrine.")

With donations from people around the island, the shrine construction project went forward and dot architects was hired to design it. This was an entirely unforeseen development for us. Structural engineer Eisuke Mitsuda ran with the project's utterly fictitious premise and came up with a radical addition to the structural design: since the sculpture itself expanded and contracted, so should the shrine housing it. By mounting the foundation on hydraulic jacks, he made it possible to move the shrine up and down. When the sculpture isn't in motion the roof remains in low position so as not to block the view of Mt. Dounzan behind it, but when the sculpture is moving the entire roof can be raised. Instead of a mobile home, a mobile shrine. After it was built, the Beat Shrine Construction Association changed its name to the Beat Shrine Preservation Association.

The process of design always demands objective assessments. Answers must be found to accommodate the manifold conditions at hand: the purpose of the structure, the desires of the users, laws and regulations, costs, and any number of technical issues. Whether or not there is a story behind it, a work of architecture is a standalone entity. If it's a good piece of work, perhaps it needs no backstory. But I think architecture should have the capacity to incorporate the unforeseen, so that a tale like the one of the bell dug out of the ground can become part of our understanding of the meaning of the structure. As cultural anthropologist Sayaka Ogawa put it, "Gossip is the most primitive form of media."

Several years ago I had a chat with an 83-year-old (or so he claimed) gentleman in the park in front of our office in Kitakagaya, Osaka. He told me he had been born in the mountains of Tokushima on the island of Shikoku, lost his mother as a child, and that he and his siblings all left the mountains and went their separate ways. When he was young, he said, he walked barefoot even on snowy days, so he fashioned his own straw sandals by copying others and made skis out of bamboo to travel through the mountains. Back then even a motherless family received no assistance from the government. Life is good today, he said; after they built the Akashi Bridge you can drive across the sea, and expressways take you to faraway places in no time flat. It's like a manga, like a dream. Thanks to the Labor Standards Law, workers' conditions are unbelievably better. And it's easier than ever to buy a bicycle. "I've got diabetes, had heart bypass surgery, stomach, colon, and liver cancer, and glaucoma and cataracts in my eyes. But my childhood was so tough, I'm fine now!" he laughed. He'd worked at all kinds of jobs—logging in an isolated area of Nara and hauling the logs over the mountain to the nearest village; firing bazookas and mortars in the Self-Defense Force; working in a steel mill. Until recently, he said, he had a job as a gateball referee, but quit because he didn't like the responsibility. And, he added, he sings all the time. His story was so fascinating that I started writing it down as soon as I got back to the office. That little chat touched on so many important things—welfare, medical care, aging, work, neighborly relations—as well as conveying how, through various kinds of effort, he had overcome his past poverty and other travails. You could say that our world has expanded and that life is indeed like a dream today, as the gentleman put it, yet new problems continue to crop up one after another.

An acquaintance of mine got a job renovating a house inhabited by an elderly person living alone. Since the resident couldn't stay there while the work was in progress, she had to lodge at another location for several days. In just those few days she developed symptoms of dementia. The house she had lived in for so long had become her entire world, no doubt. If I go to the fish shop that fellow will be there; that child is wearing the clothes I patched; that plant is the one I used to water . . . If she had been able to extend her territory to the neighborhood at large, it might have mitigated the progress of her dementia. Even if it advanced, she might have been able to live freely in her neighborhood without getting locked up in a nursing home. Isn't it important to be connected with places as one is with other people, like stars in a constellation? I think the future of the towns and villages we live in hinges on whether we can create territory that facilitates such connections.

We are currently sharing a 750-square-meter cooperative studio space as one of seven teams engaged in diverse pursuits—among them art, alternative media, archiving, architecture, community studies, nonprofit activities, design, woodworking, and a fab lab. Coop Kitakagaya occupies a renovated former furniture factory. In addition to each team's rooms there are two 150-square-meter areas that can be used as work or event spaces.

The Kitakagaya district of Osaka's Suminoe Ward, where the Coop is located, once was home to a thriving shipbuilding industry that was an economic mainstay of modern-day Osaka. With the transformation of Japan's industrial structure, however, the factories moved elsewhere or closed down and the area lost much of its vitality. At one time many thousands of shipyard workers lived here, and the neighborhood boasted five coffee shops. But the last of those closed five years ago, and empty houses and vacant lots abound. Chishima Real Estate Co., which owns many of these properties, makes money by leasing land and buildings. But when a tenant moves or dies and a lot with a house on it reverts to the owner, the age of the structure and the cost of upkeep make it prohibitive to rent out again. The company habitually converted such properties into coin parking lots, but a neighborhood full of parking lots rapidly loses its appeal. So since 2003 Chishima has been operating the former shipyard site as an experimental art venue, Creative Center Osaka. More recently it converted a former steel processing plant and warehouse into a huge storehouse for large sculptures, Mega Art Storage Kitakagaya (MASK), which opens to the public once a year so people from all over can enjoy the art inside. Also, to put smaller vacant houses or lots to use, the company began renting them out to artists and designers without any contractual requirement to return them to their original state when they left. Whenever we lease a conventional rental property, our relationship to the space feels strained and distant, since we hesitate to even pound nails in the wall due to the restore-to-previous-state stipulation. Units originally built as housing do not lend themselves to use as studios for artists or craftspeople. Thanks to the low rent and the lack of a restoration requirement in Kitakagaya, the area is gradually filling with artists and designers. The year 2009 saw the launch of the Kitakagaya Creative Village project with the aim of linking together local studios that until then had led somewhat isolated existences.

One of these vacant buildings had been occupied by Chidori Bunka Housing, a two-story apartment house with retail businesses on the ground floor—a café, barber shop, and other stores. Despite the name Bunka ("Culture"), the second floor was actually a warren of tiny rooms rented by laborers. The building was quite old, and the lady who ran the café on the ground floor told us what it was like when the shipyard was still in business. She said that many foreigners lived in the area for brief periods, and that they would take the dustcloths hanging to dry in front of the shop and use them as hand towels at the public bathhouse. If she put the washing machine outside it would quickly disappear, too, so she had to lock it down with a

chain. Fires were so frequent that locals often remarked, "Kagaya's burning again." It was a bustling and somewhat dangerous place. Even more recently, someone broke the window of a friend's car and made off with all his equipment. No doubt it got sold somewhere.

It was rumored that a ship's carpenter had built Chidori Bunka Housing with shipbuilding materials and scraps from a demolition site. Lintels and columns were used for the beams and wall frames, and the whole thing seemed on the verge of collapsing. But when the last tenant, a 92-year-old living alone, was removed by her family and the building became completely vacant, we were offered an opportunity to put it to use. Renamed Chidori Bunka, it would be jointly run by four parties: Chishima Real Estate, graf (creative direction), dot architects (design and management), and Kotaro Konishi (management). Today the same members continue to run it, a work in progress of trial-and-error operations and projects.

Chidori Bunka is a three-minute walk from our office. Although we were already working in Kitakagaya, we'd had no real opportunity to interact with neighboring residents or workers in the factories. Now we are attempting to open up some territory in Kitakagaya by providing a neighborhood spot with a new feel, where people who live and work here can find the space and time to intermingle freely. By territory I don't mean a sense of "turf," but a place outside the home where anyone can feel comfortable. For that purpose we have planned a mix of functions. The ground floor has a cafeteria, bar, shop, and atrium (a space open to all that can be used for events, or as a library, etc.). The second floor contains six small gallery spaces (collectively known as the Room Project) operated by the Chishima Foundation for Creative Osaka. Behind the building is a community garden run by the nonprofit Co.to.hana. Just recently renovation was completed on an unused section known as Unit B, opening up space for a larger gallery and nine tenants. It's already occupied by artist studios, a deli operated by the community garden, and a yoga classroom. The Chidori Bunka Cafeteria is open to the public as well as serving as a sort of company cafeteria for people working at Coop Kitakagaya and elsewhere in the neighborhood. The bar is run by myself, Wataru Doi, and Hidefumi Terada of dot architects along with Keigo Mikajiri of contact Gonzo, with occasional participation by other architects, designers and artists as guest bartenders. Our clientele is mostly from the neighborhood, and the conversations are always varied and interesting.

Overseas there are "materials banks" that buy and sell old building materials in a large space resembling a home improvement center. Since demolished buildings in Kitakagaya continue to be a generous source of old fixtures and hardware, we opened a materials bank on the ground floor of Chidori Bunka so that instead of discarding these items, we could recycle them in the community for use in renovating studios and homes. However, such materials have proven to be a hard sell, so now we also carry things like artists' goods and the unusual objects Mikajiri brings back from his performance tours abroad. By engaging not only in the design but also

the operation of the place, I meet all kinds of people. Our regulars get to expand their territory, and we get to expand our opportunities to make the acquaintance of people who just happened to drop by. It's nice to have several roles to play in one's workplace as I do by being a bartender, not just an architect. It's expected that over time Chidori Bunka will change in a number of ways. I hope we can keep experimenting together with many different people on many different projects—gardens, eateries, bars, shops, libraries, events, art—whatever comes to mind, without limiting ourselves. Above all, I want it to be fun.

City Bus

While helping manage Chidori Bunka, I also moonlight as a bartender there once or twice a month. The idea of an architect tending bar while working on designs may sound frivolous to some. But the Chidori Bunka Cafeteria is currently run by video engineer Kotaro Konishi and artist Rie Mochizuki along with Yumi Ishimoto, an actor formerly with the Ishinha theater company who used to prepare meals for the troupe. Keigo Mikajiri of the performance art group contact Gonzo manages the shop. So quite a few people here are engaged in tasks that have nothing to do with their particular profession.

Some time ago we raised slime mold in our office. Slime mold, I'm told, does not adapt its entire life process to its current habitat. Some percent of its behavior serves no survival function—in other word, it's playing, according to such experts as Professor Toshiyuki Nakagaki, a slime mold researcher at Hokkaido University, and Professor Masahiro Ueda of Osaka University. The reason, they explain, is that when the environment undergoes dramatic change, even if most of the organisms in a slime mold can no longer function, the others that seem to be "playing" can adapt and survive in the new environment. That's not to say that my colleagues and I are tending bar in case the time comes when we can't make a living at architecture. By expanding our horizons through multiple job descriptions instead of limiting ourselves to design, we are looking for more opportunities to interact with our environment and apply those experiences to our architecture work. As the naturalist Kumagusu Minakata (1867-1941) wrote:

> When it comes to *Comatricha nigra* and *C. laxa*, or *Trichia affinis*, *T. persimilis*,
> *T. favoginea* and *T. scabra*, or *Stemonitis herbatica* etc., few are clearly defined
> species; a great many are intermediate entities that defy classification, so that
> one despairs over determining if *Stemonitis fusca*, *St. splendens*, and *St. ferru-*
> *ginea*, for example, are species, or varieties, or variants. There are also count-
> less intermediate varieties. The more one studies the more one understands that

a key to scholarship is recognizing that the natural world is full of things that cannot be conclusively identified by species, genus, and so on. (From *Complete Works of Kumagusu Minakata, Supplementary Vol. 1*, Heibonsha, 1974)

Minakata is saying that rather than attempt to classify fungi into groups, we should focus on each one as an individual entity. When I tend bar, I meet individuals—Mr. X, Ms. Y—not a collective category of "locals." I am reminded of what Ryuta Imafuku said when I heard him talk about John Cage, quoting from *John Cage, For the Birds*:

> Stony Point [where Cage lived] was a treasure trove of mushrooms of all kinds. "The more you know them, the less sure you feel about identifying them. Each one is itself. Each mushroom is what it is—its own center. It's useless to pretend to know mushrooms. They escape your erudition."

Cage apparently grew interested in mushrooms because "mushroom" appeared right above "music" in his dictionary. Later he helped found the New York Mycological Society, and was known as a serious mycologist. Behind his use of chance and improvisation in music, mushrooms grow. Besides design work, dot architects has engaged in a fair number of projects involving construction or fabrication. What's more, we often collaborate with kindred spirits among our acquaintances, not only with members of the same office. And though we're often told to stop showing up at work sites and getting in the way, these sites are where we come up with all sorts of ideas and find ourselves pushed in more interesting directions. The process itself is a form of play for us. Sometimes we build something just to demolish it again. That may sound like a waste of time and effort, but we can't help it—it's fun. You commit mind and body to something that might be considered a sort of dissipation, that can't be assigned a monetary value. You get to enjoy the unique energy, groove, and weirdness of a work site, make adjustments to whatever comes up on the fly, improvise on the spot. Before starting work at a site, we and our colleagues play for a bit—frisbee, catch and the like. Then we get down to work as if it were a continuation of the frisbee session. If anything, we'd like play and work to be seamless so we can treat architecture entirely as an act of play. When I was becoming something of a street vendor myself, I learned about the street vendors of Tanzania from cultural anthropologist Sayaka Ogawa, who has studied them extensively. They are not systematically organized, but while each individual pursues his own self-interest, they also take one another's needs into consideration when absolutely

necessary. They form a sort of guild, but that guild is like the route map for one of the local "city buses" that anybody can hop on or off anywhere, anytime. Defying any notion of organization, with new things

constantly replacing old, this loose arrangement makes it possible to shift direction and modify one's way of life as circumstances dictate. I think this flexible style of ad-hoc adaptation is much more interesting than a formal decision-making system. Although dot architects is a small organization, we want to emulate the city bus model as much as possible. Once we tried to hold near-mandatory daily meetings to report on each day's work assignments, but you could see the life drain out of the entire staff. That's just the type of people who make up dot architects. In our architecture work we want to foster an environment in which we can avoid a fixed office style or brand, altering our approach on the spot as need be, staying open to all possibilities, just like a slime mold or a city bus. That's why I'm fine with mixing drinks behind a counter. A single gin and tonic has its own architecture.

Party

Twenty years ago, dot architects got its start creating the decor for a party at a club in Kobe. We hauled two tons of rebar downstairs to the basement club just for that one-night event. For two days we worked and slept there while we built a huge cage-like space out of rebar and tie wire, then stayed on for the party. The next morning we took apart the rebar and removed it, restoring the club to its original state. Some time later, for a three-day party that was something like a sequel to the first one, we brought in lumber, partied at night, then rearranged the wood fixtures the next day, in this way creating a different space every night. For three days we repeatedly altered the space, barely getting any sleep in the process. Then we tore it all down and restored the club as before.

At the Port City Kobe Art Festival held in the autumn of 2017, we opened a temporary outdoor club, "Under the Bridge," directly beneath Kobe Ohashi Bridge, a massive span that links the mainland to the artificial Port Island. With the help of friends who run a small live music and gallery space in Kobe and some DJs with Kobe roots, we sent sounds wafting over the harbor into the autumn night every weekend for a month. The sundry people who showed up seemed to enjoy themselves, whether dancing wildly or just relaxing and listening to the music.

The party progressed amid a very dynamic ambience of DJs and musicians coming and going, visitors moving around in various ways, and the venue itself changing in appearance. A temporary space that, like this one, will ultimately vanish without a trace, can embrace elements of chance, energy and improvisation that produce a mood of euphoria and a place anyone can feel at home.

In *TAZ: The Temporary Autonomous Zone, Ontological Anarchy, Poetic Terrorism*, Hakim Bey elaborates on a quote from Stephen Pearl Andrews in *The Science of Society* as follows:

Whether open only to a few friends, like a dinner party, or to thousands of celebrants, like a Be-In, the party is always "open" because it is not "ordered"; it may be planned, but unless it "*happens*" it's a failure. The element of spontaneity is crucial.

 The essence of the party: face-to-face, a group of humans synergize their efforts to realize mutual desires, whether for good food and cheer, dance, conversation, the arts of life; perhaps even for erotic pleasure, or to create a communal artwork, or to attain the very transport of bliss [. . .] —or else, in Kropotkin's terms, a basic biological drive to "mutual aid."

Today we are rapidly losing opportunities to hold parties as Bey describes them. We get together at bars or in karaoke boxes, usually for a prearranged purpose; moreover, such places charge money for access. The kind of party described above, by contrast, is a gathering of people (anywhere from two to a huge crowd) who may vary in their objectives, yet all can find a comfort zone there and comport themselves in ways having nothing to do with their role in society. There is no goal in this. From day to day, from hour to hour, relationships may shift around and the expression of different selves is permitted. When we examine a problem facing society and try to address it through architecture, even if we find a solution and make it work, as often as not the same problem recurs, since it's still the same society that gave rise to the problem. A temporary alternative space like a party allows us to toss off the role assigned us in everyday life, encourages different (in various senses) kinds of contact, and adds variation to our lives. Recently I've been thinking that amenability to partying might be one indicator of a good work of architecture. There is a genre of music called "house," so named apparently because people enjoyed the sounds—an extension of the disco music of the day—with friends in their homes. Like house music, party spaces are not meant to be exclusively outside the home. I'd like to design houses as well as other buildings that I can visualize as places to party.

 A friend once told me about having the movie-like experience of riding in the back of a pickup truck driven by a quarterback, arriving at a house where a party was in full swing while the parents were away, and puking into an urn atop a chest of drawers. Now that's a party.

UmakiCamp
UmakiCamp
2013

《UmakiCamp》は4カ月かけて建設された。ドットアーキテクツのメンバーだった向井達也が常駐し、ひたすらつくり続け、ほかのメンバーは毎週末小豆島に通っていた。向井くんはご近所の方々からいっぺんに可愛がってもらっていた。現場の終盤、切羽詰まった際には、ご近所の方々で向井くんの手を止めないように、作業中に話しかけないよう申し合わせていたそうだ。向井くんは今、小豆島町の職員となり、家族と犬と一緒に島で暮らしている。

It took four months to build UmakiCamp. Tatsuya Mukai, a member of dot architects, took up full-time residence and continued to work on it, while other members visited Shodoshima every weekend. Mukai became a favorite of the neighbors. When he was working feverishly to complete the site, they took care to avoid distracting him. Mukai now works for the town of Shodoshima and lives on the island with his family and dog.

もものうらビレッジ三角庵
Momonoura Village Sankakuan
2017

アトリエ・ワンから声をかけていただき、「もものうらビレッジ」というプロジェクトに関わる機会をいただいた。そこに生えている木を切って資材とし、一般の参加者を募るサマースクールで建設するという、現代の建設システムとは大きく異なるプロセスを展開するとても面白いプロジェクト。元ドットアーキテクツの安川雄基も加わって建設した。翌年に再訪した際に、建築と同じ形の小さな鳥屋を設置した。鳥はまだ来ない。

Atelier Bow-Wow invited us to participate in a project called Momonoura Village. We were to build a tiny house as part of a summer school open to the general public, felling trees on the site for use as construction materials. This process, so different from today's standard construction system, made the project very intriguing. Former dot architects member Yuki Yasukawa joined us in the construction work. When we visited the site the following year, we added a tiny birdhouse in the same shape as the structure we had built. So far, no birds have moved in.

瀬戸内国際芸術祭2016 -Creator in Residence-「木道」
Setouchi Triennale 2016 Creator in Residence: Boardwalk
2016

資材調達のために、敷地の裏山の所有者の方と一緒に木を切り倒しに行った。私たちは林業のプロではないし、整備されたわけでもない山でのチェーンソーで切った木が他の木に引っ掛かってしまい、木にロープを掛けて引っ張り倒している。UMA / design farmの原田祐馬さんも一緒に引っ張っている。山で切り倒した後は、そのまま海辺の広場まで運び、皮を剥いでの断し、杭になるように削りだした。いつも何か面白い材料がないか見ている。

To obtain the lumber for our project, we went out with the owner of the forest on the mountain behind our site and felled trees there. We aren't forestry professionals, nor was the forest maintained, so when we cut through the trees with a chain saw they would get caught on other trees and we would have to tie a rope around them and pull them down. Yuma Harada of UMA/design farm helped us out. After taking the trees down we hauled them to an open lot by the sea, where we stripped off their bark and saved them up into posts. We are always looking for interesting materials to work with.

en[縁] : アート・オブ・ネクサス
—— 第15回ヴェネチア・ビエンナーレ国際建築展
en[縁]: Art of Nexus—15th International Architecture Exhibition of the Venice Biennale
2016

ヴェネチアで《UmakiCamp》の一部を原寸大で建てることになったため、ハンドツールをキャスター付き工具箱ひとつに詰め込んで飛行機で運んだ。日本館の前は枝振りの良い木が生えているので、その下を《作業場》にしてガンガンつくった。日本館の設営をしていたイタリア人に「建築家が来ると言われていたがお前たちは何者だ?」と言われた。インド・ムンバイでル・コルビュジエが建てたモダンな学校に馴染めず、現地の人が木の下を教室にしていた写真を思い出す。

Having decided to reconstruct a full-size section of UmakiCamp in Venice, we packed all our hand tools in a single toolbox on casters and brought it on the plane with us. We set up our work tables under a tree with nicely shaped branches in front of the Japan Pavilion and noisily banged the thing together. An Italian who was setting up the pavilion said, "We were told there would be architects coming, but who are you guys?" I was reminded of a photo of people in India who didn't feel comfortable in a modern school designed by Le Corbusier, so they held their classes under a tree.

地域に潜るアジア：参加するオープン・ラボラトリー
Open Call Laboratory: An Exploration into Social Anthropology in Asia
2014

行先では材をどこで調達するかをまず考える。地元の方々に使える材がないかを尋ね、ホームセンターの場所をおさえる。この現場では竹林を整備するボランティアの方々と竹を切り出し、木置の土砂崩れにようでなぎ倒された斜面に引っかかっている木を車で引きずり下ろした。その場で枝を払い、皮を剥ぎ、長さを整え、1/1のモックアップをつくって構造の強度や空間のスケールを確認する。資材調達は宝探しのようだ。

First we had to figure out how to procure materials at our destination. We asked local contacts if they had materials we could use, and ascertained the location of a home improvement center. At the site we cut down bamboo with the help of volunteers who maintained a bamboo grove there, and used a truck to drag down trees that were lying on the hillside after being knocked flat by a rain-induced mudslide. We lopped off the branches and stripped the bark on the spot, cut the logs to the proper length, and built a 1:1 mockup to check the strength and spatial scale of the structure. Procuring materials is a lot like a treasure hunt.

鉄道芸術祭 vol.5 クロージングイベント「これからの、もうひとつの電車」
Railway Art Festival vol.5: Closing Event "Alternative Train of the Future"
2015

ホンマタカシさんプロデュースの展覧会に設営で参加。黒田益朗、小山友也、NAZE、PUGMENT、蓮沼執太、マティアス・ヴェルムカ&ミーシャ・ラインカウフ といった面白い方々が参加していた。最終日には、ホンマさんのアイデアで展覧会そのものを解体するパフォーマンスが行われ、私たちも解体道具を持って参加。必死でつくったものを一瞬で破壊。ホンマさんの写真の上にNAZEさんのグラフィティが重なっていて凄くかっこいい。

We worked on the setup of an exhibition produced by Takashi Homma. The other participants were interesting people like Masuo Kuroda, Yuya Koyama, NAZE, PUGMENT, Shuta Hasunuma, and Matthias Wermke & Mischa Leinkauf. It was Homma's idea to end the final day with a performance in which the exhibition itself was dismantled, so we brought demolition tools and joined in. The things we'd taken so much trouble to build were dismantled in no time. NAZE covered Homma's photographs with some very cool graffiti.

contact Gonzo「ゴンゾ解體新書（かいたいしんしょ）」13分間東屋

contact Gonzo: *Gonzo Kaitai Shinsho* 13-minute Azumaya

2016

アーティストのcontact Gonzoが大阪市の「咲くやこの花賞」を受賞した際に行われたイベントに参加。

ダンサーやアーティストがcontact Gonzoを解釈し直してパフォーマンスを行った。私たちは角材とゴムを用い、人が柱となることで東屋をつくった。さらにそのゴムにさまざまな物を引っ掛け、ゴムや角材を流れる力を変化させていく。東屋が破綻しないようにそれぞれの身体のふるまいを感じながらバランスをとった。次に向けて道具は事務所に置いてある。

We participated in an event organized on the occasion of the artist group contact Gonzo's receipt of Osaka City's Sakuyakonohana Award. Dancers and artists performed their interpretations of contact Gonzo's work. Using square timber and rubber bands, we built an *azumaya*-style gazebo in which human bodies served as the pillars. We then hung various items on the rubber to vary the tension passing through the rubber and wood. Each body responded intuitively to find a balance to prevent the structure from collapsing. The materials are stored in our office in anticipation of the next such opportunity.

KYOTO EXPERIMENT 2017
神里雄大／岡崎藝術座《バルパライソの長い坂を下る話》

KYOTO EXPERIMENT 2017: Yudai Kamisato/Okazaki Art Theatre, *The Story of Descending the Long Slopes of Valparaiso*

2017

作家、舞台演出家である神里雄大さんの「バルパライソの長い坂を下る話」の舞台美術を担当。この作品で神里さんは第62回岸田國士戯曲賞を受賞された。ここでは客席に脚本に登場するさまざまなオブジェクトを配置し、お客さんが好きな場所で演劇を楽しめるようになっている。神里さんは、この後一緒に石垣島を旅行した。建築家の藤村龍至さん、北加賀屋の面々とも一緒で、ずっと泡盛を飲んでいた。

We handled the set design for playwright/director Yudai Kamisato's play *The Story of Descending the Long Slopes of Valparaiso*, for which he received the 62nd Kishida Prize for Drama. We placed various objects that appear in the script in the seating area and let the audience sit wherever they liked. Afterward Kamisato traveled with us to Ishigaki Island. Together with architects Ryuji Fujimura and Koji Kakiuchi and a group of people from Kitakagaya, we spent the whole time drinking *awamori* liquor.

dot architects **Projects**

名前	完了年	用途	所在地・計画地	設計・施工・製作	常設・仮設	協働
CHURCH	1998	仮設結婚式場	大阪府東大阪市	設計・施工	仮設	浅野大輔、中島康博
Release the tension1	1998	クラブイベント会場	兵庫県神戸市	設計・施工	仮設	浅野大輔、中島康博
Release the tension2	1998	クラブイベント会場	兵庫県神戸市	設計・施工	仮設	浅野大輔、中島康博
Release the tension3	1999	クラブイベント会場	兵庫県神戸市	設計・施工	仮設	浅野大輔、中島康博
Release the tension4	1999	クラブイベント会場	兵庫県神戸市	設計・施工	仮設	浅野大輔、中島康博
OTOYA WC	1999	店舗	兵庫県神戸市	設計・施工	常設	浅野大輔、中島康博
KAWAKABE	2000	店舗	兵庫県神戸市	設計・施工	常設	浅野大輔、中島康博
grassroots1	2000	クラブイベント会場	兵庫県神戸市	設計・施工	仮設	
ランジェリーshop	2000	クラブイベント会場	兵庫県神戸市	設計・施工	仮設	
Tgroup	2000	クラブイベント会場	兵庫県神戸市	設計・施工	常設	
ghetto	2001	店舗	兵庫県神戸市	設計・施工	常設	
grassroots2	2001	クラブイベント会場	兵庫県神戸市	設計・施工	仮設	
grassroots3	2001	クラブイベント会場	兵庫県神戸市	設計・施工	仮設	
catenaube	2002	店舗	兵庫県神戸市	設計・施工	常設	
lecce	2002	店舗	兵庫県神戸市	設計・施工	常設	
かべノキてんじょう	2002	店舗	兵庫県神戸市	設計	仮設	小西小多郎、武中大輔
BAR JAZZ	2003	店舗	大阪府大阪市	設計・部分施工	常設	
湊町アンダーグラウンドKPJ	2003	展覧会会場	大阪府大阪市	設計・施工	仮設	寺尾茂秀、寺久保茂生
KUNYAKUNYANOTANA	2003	家具	大阪府大阪市	設計・製作		寺尾茂秀
SARASWATI	2003	店舗	兵庫県西宮市	設計	常設	
高橋匡太 third dimention	2003	舞台美術	東京都	施工	仮設	
森本さんの机	2003	家具		設計	-	
wallstream	2004	ショウルーム	大阪府大阪市	設計・施工	仮設	
POOL	2004	パフォーマンス会場	新世界BRIDGE	設計・施工	仮設	武中大輔
grassroots4	2004	クラブイベント会場	兵庫県神戸市	設計・施工	仮設	
高橋匡太 Light Cylinder Project	2004	パフォーマンス会場	兵庫県神戸市	設計・施工	仮設	
ipsi	2004	インスタレーション	タマダプロジェクトアートスペース	施工	仮設	
1room	2004	内装	神戸アートビレッジセンター	設計	仮設	大創工務店
チャンスセンター	2004	店舗	兵庫県神戸市	設計	常設	大創工務店
桂	2004	店舗	兵庫県神戸市	設計	常設	
高橋匡太 High Energy Field	2004	インスタレーション	KPO＋リソグラフ大阪	施工	仮設	武中大輔
NI-MA	2004	住宅(改修)	兵庫県神戸市	設計	常設	
Twinkle moon	2004	店舗	兵庫県神戸市	設計	常設	大創工務店
KAVCチケットカウンター	2005	家具	神戸アートビレッジセンター	設計	常設	
武庫山裾展示板	2005	看板	兵庫県宝塚市	設計	常設	
POOL2	2005	パフォーマンス会場	新世界BRIDGE	施工	仮設	

池田 藍（いけだ・あい）
Ai Ikeda

1979年奈良県生まれ。奈良女子大学生活環境学部卒。大阪工業技術専門学校夜間部卒。イーストロンドン大学卒。ICU architects office、アーバンフォルム建築研究所を経て独立後、ドットアーキテクツ参画。

Born in Nara, Japan in 1979.
Graduated from the Faculty of Human Life & Environment at Nara Women's University, the Osaka College of Technology, and the University of East London, UK. Worked for ICU architects office and Urban-form architects office, then established her own practice before joining dot architects.

宮地 敬子（みやち・けいこ）
Keiko Miyachi

1982年兵庫県生まれ。京都造形芸術大学空間演出デザイン学科卒。京都造形芸術大学勤務を経てフリーランスで活動後、ドットアーキテクツ参画。

Born in Hyogo, Japan in 1982.
Graduated from the Department of Spatial Design, Faculty of Art and Design at Kyoto University of Art and Design. Worked at Kyoto University of Art and Design, then went freelance before joining dot architects.

石田 知弘（いしだ・ともひろ）
Tomohiro Ishida

1994年島根県生まれ。滋賀県立大学大学院環境科学研究科修士課程修了後、ドットアーキテクツ参画。

Born in Shimane, Japan in 1994.
Received a master's degree in the Division of Environmental Planning at The University of Shiga Prefecture, then joined dot architects.

Former members

大東 翼（おおひがし・たすく）
Tasuku Ohigashi

安川 雄基（やすかわ・ゆうき）
Yuki Yasukawa

向井 達也（むかい・たつや）
Tatsuya Mukai

菊地 球真（きくち・たくま）
Takuma Kikuchi

家成 俊勝（いえなり・としかつ）
Toshikatsu Ienari

1974年兵庫県生まれ。関西大学法学部法律学科卒。
大阪工業技術専門学校夜間部卒。
・京都芸術大学空間演出デザイン学科教授

Born in Hyogo, Japan in 1974.
Graduated from the Department of Law, Faculty of Law at Kansai University, and the Osaka College of Technology.
Co-founded dot architects in 2004.
Currently professor at Kyoto University of Art and Design.

赤代 武志（しゃくしろ・たけし）
Takeshi Shakushiro

1974年兵庫県生まれ。神戸芸術工科大学芸術工学部環境デザイン学科卒。
北村陸夫＋ズーム計画工房、宮本佳明建築設計事務所を経て設計活動を開始。
・大阪工業技術専門学校 特任教員
・京都芸術大学環境デザイン学科非常勤講師
・大阪市立大学生活科学部居住環境学科非常勤講師

Born in Hyogo, Japan in 1974.
Graduated from the Department of Environmental Design, Faculty of Design at Kobe Design University.
Worked at Rikuo Kitamura + Zoom Architect & Associates and Katsuhiro Miyamoto & Associates.
Co-founded dot architects in 2004.
Currently lecturer at Osaka College of Technology, Kyoto University of Art and Design, and Osaka City University.

土井 亘（どい・わたる）
Wataru Doi

1987年神奈川県生まれ。慶應義塾大学政策・メディア研究科修士課程修了。studio mumbai architectsを経てドットアーキテクツ参画。

Born in Kanagawa, Japan in 1987.
Received a master's degree in Media and Governance at Keio University.
Worked at Studio Mumbai Architects, then joined dot architects.

寺田 英史（てらだ・ひでふみ）
Hidefumi Terada

1990年埼玉県生まれ。横浜国立大学大学院建築都市スクールY-GSA修士課程修了後、ドットアーキテクツ参画。

Born in Saitama, Japan in 1990.
Received a master's degree in Architectural and Urban Design at Yokohama Graduate School of Architecture, then joined dot architects.

パーティー